D0284585

THE HARD CROWD

Essays 2000–2020

Rachel Kushner

Scribner

New York   London   Toronto   Sydney   New Delhi

Scribner
An Imprint of Simon & Schuster, Inc.
1230 Avenue of the Americas
New York, NY 10020

First Scribner hardcover edition April 2021

The epigraph on page vii is from *The Passion According to G.H.* by Clarice Lispector, translated by Idra Novey.

SCRIBNER and design are registered trademarks of The Gale Group, Inc., used under license by Simon & Schuster, Inc., the publisher of this work.

For information about special discounts for bulk purchases, please contact Simon & Schuster Special Sales at 1-866-506-1949 or business@simonandschuster.com.

The Simon & Schuster Speakers Bureau can bring authors to your live event. For more information or to book an event, contact the Simon & Schuster Speakers Bureau at 1-866-248-3049 or visit our website at www.simonspeakers.com.

Interior design by Wendy Blum

Manufactured in the United States of America

1   3   5   7   9   10   8   6   4   2

Library of Congress Cataloging-in-Publication Data has been applied for.

ISBN 978-1-9821-5769-2
ISBN 978-1-9821-5771-5 (ebook)

This book is for Peter Kushner and Pinky Drosten Kushner.

What others get from me is then reflected back onto me, and forms the atmosphere called: "I."

CONTENTS

GIRL ON A MOTORCYCLE

often hid in the garage after I was kicked outside to play on summer days. Its attractions for a young child were a wooden-wheeled scooter I rode around on the smooth concrete floor; stacks of crated peaches, there for pilfering until my mother got around to her canning; and a 1955 Vincent Black Shadow. The Vincent was my father's motorcycle, which he had bought in England in 1965, three years before I was born. My parents and older brother, just a baby, were living in London, in a cold-water flat in Kentish Town, then working class, where a famous theorist of the working class—Karl Marx—also once lived. While my twenty-two-year-old mother was upstairs boiling diapers on the stove (in a pot she filled from a common spigot in the hall), my father spent his days working on his motorcycle on the street in front of their building. When it was too dark to continue work on the bike, he went to the pub to read books, as the electricity in my parents' flat ran on a coin-operated meter and was prohibitively dear, at least for them. My father still claims that pub culture and class consciousness go hand in hand, because everyone went to the bar for the free electricity. (By "everyone," I believe he means men.) But, as the story goes in our family, on Guy Fawkes Night my father was home with my mother, watching out the window as people dragged unwanted furniture and other junk to a blazing bonfire in the street, in keeping with the custom of the holiday, which commemorates Guy Fawkes's attempt to blow up Parliament, in 1605. When a woman pushed an empty baby pram toward the fire, my mother handed my brother to my father and ran downstairs to retrieve it. She wanted it so badly that she was in tears as she pleaded with the woman not to burn it. The woman relented and gave my mother the pram. It was a Silver Cross—a luxury make—but dirty and with a stretched spring that caused it to list to one side. My mother was thrilled with her lopsided hooptie, and she would push my brother down to Regent's Park while my father endlessly tinkered with his Vincent.

On occasion, my father rode the Vincent out to the Ace Cafe, a twenty-four-hour roadhouse diner with a giant neon sign, where the phenomenon of "café racing" was popularized. A Vincent Black Shadow was an exotic bike at the Ace, where people mostly had Triumphs, BSAs, and Nortons, tricked out with drop bars and rearsets, but the Vincent was a very fast bike in its day, with a huge (1,000 cc) motor. The first time my dad rode out to the Ace, which was on a ring road in northwest London, an argument was taking place out front, where bikes were lined up in gleaming rows. Some misguided troublemaker was defending the Mods (the Ace was strictly a Rocker scene). Mary Quant and the fashion world had claimed the Mods and their dandyish, androgynous look, their Vespas and Lambrettas, as an ascendant trend—one that threatened to overtake the Rockers as the image of cool. My father asked one of the Rockers, "So what's this about?" The guy said of the Mods, "They're fucking *women* is what!"

The Rockers were men and needed you to know it. The Mods were women. And women were also women, pushing prams. It was all before my time but loomed large in my imagination, out there in the garage. What was I? A child who coveted my father's motorcycle.

My parents moved back to the United States on a Greek freighter at the end of that year, and the Vincent came with them. There's a dent in its oxidized black gas tank from where it was dropped carelessly from the freighter to a loading dock. Alone in the garage, I would lift up its green canvas cover and listen for the tick and ting of its cast-aluminum engine shifting in the summer heat. It was coated in grime, leaking murky black oil into a pan beneath its motor, but even lodged on its center stand, both wheels off the ground, and only started as an annual event, to me it seemed an animate thing. My older brother couldn't have cared less about the difference between monkey and Allen wrenches; it was me who was willing to stand in the rain as the riders in the vintage British rally passed, my mother and me sinking into the mud on the side of the road, and me, at seven, computing that engine oil under the nails, the ability to kick-start a four-stroke or handle a suicide clutch—these were not just skills but *character*.

In the 1968 Anglo-French film *Girl on a Motorcycle*, Alain Delon gives Marianne Faithfull, his young mistress, a Harley-Davidson. For much of the movie she is on the bike, blissful and windblown as she cruises the European countryside. The motorcycle was a wedding gift: wheels to take her from Alsace, where she lives with her unwitting school-teacher husband, to Heidelberg, where she surrenders herself to Delon for attention and debasement (in one unintentionally camp sequence, he spanks her with a bouquet of roses).

Although we see her alone on the Harley, it's Delon who is driving her destiny. He has given her the bike for the purpose of ferrying her away from her husband and into his control. Yet there's no getting around the machine's intrinsic nature, that it is propelled by tremendous forward motion and steered by the rider. When she's on it, she's alone and moving fast. She passes through the French/German border at sunrise, wearing a tight black leather catsuit with nothing underneath, and wondering if the grinning agent will make her unzip (the film's original title was *Naked under Leather*). The agent pats her ass and waves her through. Although she goes to see Delon, theoretically she could go anywhere—tour Bavaria or jet off to Poland, while he smokes and broods, meanly handsome and alone.

Motorcycles didn't enter my own life as gifts from men or ways to travel to men, but as machines to be ridden. My first bike was a 500 cc Moto Guzzi, which eventually attracted a Moto Guzzi mechanic. The mechanic, older than I was by ten years, and with a stronger personality, turned out to be domineering and manipulative, a bit like Alain Delon is toward Marianne Faithfull. And unfortunately, like Faithfull's character in the film, I was under his influence, even if my interest in bikes—after the Guzzi I moved to Japanese street machines—was entirely my own. The mechanic helped me put together a race-ready Kawasaki Ninja for a dangerous and illegal road race that he, too, was riding in. Participating in the race meant both meeting his standards of skill and courage and embarking on a journey alone. I wanted his approval, I guess, but I also wanted to be liberated from that dynamic. Even if it's a man who sets a woman on a journey, for the duration of the journey, she's kinetic and unfettered and alone.

On a map, a thick black line indicates the Transpeninsular Highway, or Highway 1, which spans the length of Baja California—a long, variegated peninsula separated from mainland Mexico by the tepid, life-rich waters of the Sea of Cortez. Highway 1 is Baja's main highway. It was completed in 1973, a hallmark of modernization, an inaugural conjoining of north and south on a tract of land where people, separated by vast stretches of harsh desert and high mountains, had once had little communication beyond their own regions.

A thick black line on a map can be misleading for the uninitiated. When I undertook this race, in 1993, at age twenty-four, Highway 1 was regularly maintained (although without such luxuries as guardrails or painted lane dividers) only on the series of toll roads from Tijuana to Ensenada—a tiny portion of the 1,100-mile-long road. Beyond Ensenada, the paved roads were macadam poured directly on dirt, meaning there were as many dips and curves in the road as there were in the land beneath. Such road construction doesn't hold up well, and there were huge potholes scattered over the highway all the way down to the end of the peninsula, some of them gaping expanses of crumbled pavement that lasted fifty feet. The frequent and dramatic dips, called vados, could be filled with sand or water or, on a frigid desert night, a sleeping cow seeking lingering daytime warmth from the highway's blacktop. Baja is mountainous, and with a few exceptional straightaways, the road is a winding series of blind corners and hairpin turns. Many of the curves were not marked with warning signs, and the road surface was typically coated with diesel fuel that sloshed from Pemex trucks. The road could suddenly become one lane serving both directions, or turn from smooth pavement to washboard dirt, a violent switch of terrain that can cause a broken axle for the unprepared car and total disaster for a person on a motorcycle, especially one foolish enough to race down the Baja Peninsula in a single day, a trip that requires an average speed—hairpin turns, sleeping cows, and all—of over a hundred miles an hour.

This motorcycle road race, called the Cabo 1000, used to be an annual event that began in San Ysidro, the last American town before the border into Mexico, and finished in Cabo San Lucas, at the tip of the Baja Peninsula, approximately 1,080 miles south. In a car, this trip is four or five days of difficult driving, of extreme weather and road conditions. The required average I mentioned for the Cabo 1000 included slowing down through Baja's towns (an honor code that a few riders always disobeyed) and stopping for water breaks, gas, and repairs. In order to make the hundred-mile-per-hour average, on the straights a rider needed to push it over the top, and go as fast as her bike would do.

I had been working on my Ninja 600 for months in preparation for the Cabo ride. It was the perfect size bike for this: powerful but small and lithe enough to handle well on mountain curves. To increase speed and performance, I upgraded the bike with stainless-steel after-market valves, a resurfaced cylinder head, a high-performance carburetor jet kit, and a four-into-one exhaust with an unbaffled canister. I had long discussions with friends over what kind of tires to choose, weighing the pros and cons of performance and durability. I would need a reasonably soft tire for traction and tight cornering, but something too soft would be shredded halfway down the peninsula. Little details like choosing the proper tint of helmet face shield and having some sort of system for cleaning it on the ride were important. Some people went with tear-offs, plastic adhesives that a rider could pull off as each one gunked up with bugs and dirt. Wade Boyd, an Isle of Man veteran who had won the Cabo ride many times (one year infamously finishing on an almost toy-size race bike—a two-stroke 350), had an old tennis ball cut open and mounted on his handlebars that kept moist a little sponge he could retrieve and use to clean his face shield. Wade was a fabricator by profession, and his Cabo bike was loaded with custom amenities to help him win. He designed his own automatic chain luber, as well as a fiberglass double-decker gas tank that held an unbelievable eleven gallons of fuel (a typical motorcycle holds between four and six). His bike looked like a pregnant spider.

In the weeks before the race, I put up a map of Baja with pushpins marking the towns with Pemex stations. It was on the kitchen wall in the warehouse where I lived with my then boyfriend—the Moto Guzzi mechanic—and two other friends from the motorcycle scene, on Woodward Street in San Francisco. I'd heard that some Pemex stations could be closed without warning, due to shortages or the proprietor's mood. It would be necessary to carry extra fuel. I bought an auxiliary gas tank from a boating supply company in Oakland and, with the help of the boyfriend, mounted it securely on the passenger seat of my bike and plumbed a line from it to my gas tank, complete with an electric pump and lighted toggle switch on my handlebar.

The last few days of preparing the bike were hectic, and by the time my boyfriend and our housemate Peter Waymire, known as Stack (short for Stackmaster, meaning he crashed a lot), and I were ready to go, we'd been up all night, each tightening and testing everything on our bikes, and in Stack's case, putting his motor together.

We rolled out of San Francisco at six a.m., planning to arrive at the border in plenty of time to get some sleep before the race started early the next morning. Most of those doing the Cabo ride were SF locals, and since Tijuana is twelve hours south, people were towing their bikes down on trailers or in the back of flatbed trucks, in order to spare both tire tread and rider energy. None of us owned a truck, but my boyfriend had arranged to sell a 1960s Tohatsu, a rare Japanese motorcycle, to a guy in Los Angeles who agreed to pay for a Ryder truck to transport it. For the buyer of the Tohatsu, this was cheaper than paying for shipping; for us, it was a free ride halfway to the border. The warehouse where we lived was the former storage facility for an after-market motorcycle accessory company called Hap Jones and was full of old collectible Japanese stuff like this Tohatsu, as well as the ugly after-market Harley-Davidson accessories for which Hap Jones was famous. The company founder's son inherited the warehouse when his father died and, having no interest in motorcycles, rented the place to us cheaply and made no effort to claim any of the leftover stock from his father's company. My boyfriend was always trying to unload old motorcycles and Hap Jones deadstock by advertising in *Walneck's Classic Cycle Trader*, which was the most popular classifieds for vintage bikes. It became such a regular thing that he was on a first-name basis with the woman who answered the *Walneck's* phone number somewhere out in Illinois (he claimed she wanted to sleep with him, sight unseen).

It was mid-afternoon when we arrived in Los Angeles in the Ryder truck. The Tohatsu buyer lived in a chic part of West Hollywood and was standing on the curb as we pulled up. He had a meticulous *Wild Angels* sort of image, with perfectly rolled, double-height jean cuffs and a Brylcreemed pompadour. My boyfriend and Stack exchanged looks as if to say *yeah, poseur* as the guy handed over several hundred dollars for what we considered a silly little bike. It was a funny moment: there we were, our mean and scrappy road bikes unloaded from the truck, and us in duct-taped race leathers and Kevlar gloves, on our way to participate in a superdangerous, all-motorcycles-all-the-time sort of event. Meanwhile here was this other type, but also an enthusiast. He'd gone to extravagant lengths to buy an obscure machine, and with his clothes and the careful hair, he had obviously tailored his life to fit with the sort of bikes he loved. He had his thing; it was different from our thing, but we were all gearheads.

Stack had grown up in LA, and on his recommendation we went to a Middle Eastern counter on Hollywood Boulevard. We ate our falafels sitting on the sidewalk, where we could watch our motorcycles. LA was in a heat wave, and the temperature that afternoon was over 100 degrees. I was wilting in my heavy race leathers and exhausted from not sleeping the night before. When we got on the freeway heading south toward the border, we were in rush-hour traffic with 150 miles to go. Stack had been an LA motorcycle messenger, and with his seat-of-the-pants riding skills and LA freeway experience he led us on a fifty-miles-per-hour adventure riding between car lanes. Every motorcyclist splits lanes, but not at fifty miles an hour. I thought I was going to have a heart attack the entire time, waiting for someone to switch lanes and cut me off. But asking my boyfriend, who was following Stack, to slow down would have been out of the question—and the sort of situation he relished. "Ride aggressively or die in the saddle," he would have said.

At sundown we arrived in San Ysidro, a small town with a Motel 6, a Denny's across the street, a few currency exchange shacks, and a massive border station into Tijuana. My nerves were shot from the lane-splitting adventure, and the ride hadn't even started yet. I began to feel better when I spotted my friend Michelle, who was riding her Honda CBR around the Motel 6 parking lot in shorts, a bathing suit top, and sturdy motocross boots she'd enhanced with a purple felt-tipped pen. Michelle was one of three women, including me, of the twenty-nine riders participating in the race, and a skilled motorcyclist. She came along to eat with us at the Denny's, as my boyfriend talked about how he could have been a prodigy computer scientist if he'd felt like it (he made his living as a mechanic and by growing pot in our warehouse), and about how the Denny's waitress had given him "the look" when he'd taken off his helmet (his expression was "the dick eye," women everywhere—tall, short, old, young, fat, thin—always giving him the dick eye). When he got up to use the bathroom, Michelle burst out laughing. She'd had her own romantic run-in with him and was circumspect. I was embarrassed for him and having doubts of my own.

There was a riders meeting after dinner, and everyone congregated around the motel pool to hear Lee Jones, who organized the Cabo race, speak. I'm not using Lee's real name, but he was nobility in the motorcycle scene. When you signed up to go to Cabo you wrote him a check (it was a hundred dollars the year I participated). The money supposedly would go to the elementary schools of Baja, and no one ever questioned the legitimacy of Lee's philanthropic dealings. He was a stoic man with steel-gray hair and eyes to match, and he owned a motorcycle messenger service with a notorious reputation and delivery boys who looked like Glenn Danzig. People enjoyed saying that Lee was "raised by Hells Angels," and they said it with reverence, as if he'd been raised by wolves. Lee told us that if we were pulled over by federales, we were to claim no comprendo. Everyone was handed a letter written in Spanish to carry with us on the ride. It was apparently from the chamber of commerce, explaining that we were on a charity ride raising money for the children of Baja. There was talk at the meeting of how unlikely it was this letter would prove useful: no one was planning to pull over if summoned by a federale. A raceworthy bike can easily outrun a cop—of any jurisdiction, American too, and many of these riders regularly outran cops for fun, at home in SF (on my first date with that boyfriend, he'd routed them on his dual-purpose KLR 650 by going down a steep set of steps and popping off a three-foot embankment, with me on the back). The next morning, into my race, I passed children on the side of the road, but I was going 120 mph, and they were only a blur. I assume that what the children of Baja got from our charity ride was little more than a glimpse of screaming, dust-kicking motorcycles.

There were two girls at the meeting who were there to drive the crash truck, which would carry everyone's belongings to Cabo San Lucas and pick up bikes that broke down or wrecked along Highway 1. A guy whose name I can't recall accompanied the crash truck girls. I forget his name because we immediately started calling him Reggae on the River, after a summer music festival on the Eel River that attracts laid-back, long-haired guys like this one. Reggae on the River had originally planned on riding in the race, but his front brake assembly had fallen apart as he came off the San Ysidro freeway exit toward the Motel 6, and he'd destroyed his gearbox downshifting through an intersection (as well as completely melting the soles of his boots) trying to bring the bike to a stop.

After the riders' meeting, I went to bed. It was ten p.m., and the motel alarm was set to go off at three thirty a.m. My boyfriend was in the parking lot, making last-minute adjustments on his motorcycle, convinced he was going to dust infamous and favored Lee Jones and Wade Boyd. I drifted off but was woken periodically by voices outside; a former warehouse roommate of ours named Sean Crane was talking to someone about the pros and cons of synthetic engine oil. Sean had a sweet-yet-guilty, girlish smile and long, wavy hair, and he wore black race leathers with the white bones of a skeleton stitched over them. Mounted on a race bike, he looked like a visitation of death. Sean rode on the street as if he were on the racetrack: he was gifted but took huge risks. On the Cabo ride the previous year, he had been dicing with another rider, a guy from Los Angeles whom, as it turned out, no one else really knew. Sean had out-braked the other guy on a blind curve overlooking a cliff, and the other rider crashed, toppled over the cliff, and had to be airlifted to a hospital in San Diego. He ended up losing his leg. Sean kept going.

At four thirty a.m. we were lined up in the dark parking lot of the Motel 6, all twenty-nine of us revving our engines like a swarm of angry bees. There was no suggestion of sunrise, and thick fog obscured the full moon with which the race had been scheduled to coincide. I hadn't said any good lucks to friends, or much at all for that matter, as from the moment the alarm went off, the focus had been on suiting up, warming up the bike, taking care of last-minute preparations— such as ensuring that my ziplock-protected map would stay secured on the top of my gas tank—and then getting into position. People I knew had become dark, unfamiliar silhouettes in race leathers and full-face helmets, their shields down. My boyfriend pulled up next to me and gave me a deerskin-gloved thumbs-up, but I was already in my own world, overtaken by fear and some other more positive emotions— excitement—and then we were pulling out of the lot in a cacophonous group. He swerved around me and surged ahead. I was on my own and thinking, *This is where entropy and rider skill take over; this is it, I'm alone in this thing.* Those in front, doing up to 160 mph, would reach Cabo by sundown, as others rolled in all through the night, fifteen or twenty hours from now. I passed the border into Mexico and hit the first long incline up a dark mountain, my headlight slicing through the wet ocean fog. I was somewhere mid-pack and trying to stay focused, going over what I knew, what I'd been told, what to expect, how to be ready.

In the mountains between Tijuana and Ensenada, the fog was dense. The roads were slick and full of hairpin turns. By the time I reached Ensenada, I was through the worst of the fog, but the dark, sleeping city had its own set of hazards. Speed bumps were not painted as they are in the States, and I accidentally flew over a set of them going eighty miles an hour, which meant sailing through the air and then—because the suspension on the bike was dialed down for stiff and precise cornering—a very hard landing.

Fuel gets burned at an exponential rate at speeds of over 80, and gas virtually disappears when you're flying at 130. The first time I flipped my auxiliary fuel switch—a comforting blue glow among my orange-lit instruments—it was a wonderful feeling to watch the needle on my gas gauge slowly rise instead of fall, as an extra four gallons filled the Ninja's tank.

After El Rosario, the land stretched out into a lowland farming valley. Dawn was approaching, the fog dissipating into big, translucent puffs that drifted across the road, when a farmer pulled out right in front of me. He must not have seen me, in his battered pickup, a single headlight mounted and glowing dimly on the cab roof. I had to brake hard to avoid hitting him. Unfortunately, I braked on a patch of gravel. The bike got into what is known as a tank slapper, when the front wheel loses control and wobbles violently back and forth, the handlebars hitting the tank alternately. It's a situation that's impossible to control, and best just ridden out. I managed to regain control of the bike and kept going, adrenaline now coursing through me and the light getting stronger.

By the time I needed to make my first fuel stop, the sun was high. I'd been passing lumbering recreational vehicles one after the other for a couple hundred miles through the Vizcaino Desert, a place filled with Volkswagen-size boulders, some of them decorated with make-shift grave markers, candles, religious deities, and plastic flowers. I had made it to Cataviña, a barren and windblown rest stop more than a third of the way down the Baja Peninsula. When I pulled into the Pemex station, I was worried the attendant would insist on pumping my gas for me. They always do if you're driving a car, and I didn't want him spilling gas over the lip of the auxiliary tank. But after watching me take off my helmet, adjust and lube my chain, and add a half quart of oil to the motor, he knew I had an agenda of my own, and he smiled and handed me the gas nozzle. I felt good—strong and in a rhythm.

By noon I was approaching the halfway mark. I'd been passed by, and had passed, a few riders, and knew I was somewhere in the middle of the pack. Five hundred miles down the Baja Peninsula, just before Guerrero Negro, the town that spans the north/south border of Baja, is the longest uninterrupted straight on the Transpeninsular Highway. I went into it going 120, tucked down into my fairing, and rolled the throttle to its pegged position. I hit 142 miles an hour, the fastest I'd ever gone.

I could see the giant metal sculpture that marks the north/south border, a fifty-foot-tall steel-beam structure that I've heard is meant to be a bird but looks more like a grounded oil dredge. I rolled off the throttle just a touch. Up ahead on the right shoulder was a group of parked motorcycles. I recognized Wade Boyd, who should have been miles and miles ahead of me, and another guy we called Doc. A motorcyclist on the shoulder with them pulled suddenly onto the highway in front of me. Either he didn't see me or he didn't realize how fast I was going. It was someone I knew from our biker bar in San Francisco, the name of which—Zeitgeist—he had stitched into the back of his red-and-black race leathers. After many hours of solitary and intense concentration, I was pleased to see those familiar and ridiculous leathers. But then reality set in—that he was going only 30 miles an hour and I was going 130—and I was approaching in no time. I swerved out to avoid him. Just as I got around, I saw that the road took an unannounced and extremely sharp left-hand turn. There was a truck coming in the other direction, so I wouldn't be able to use up both lanes to try to corner. I was going way, way, way too fast to lean the motorcycle hard enough to cut the turn, and I didn't want to get smeared underneath trying. I opted to ride off the road.

The area beyond the road paving was a shallow, sandy ditch, which in hindsight seems unbelievably lucky—most of the way down, the road is jagged rock on one side, ocean cliff on the other, or rocks on both sides. But hitting such a radical surface change at 130 mph, even if it is sand, will have consequences, and as I left the pavement, the bike vaulted me. My recall of this event is fractured into memory pictures: I see the tire leave the road, and then I am up in midair over the bike, separated from it, high above the instruments and handlebars, and then there's a quick and violent descent to a brutal, thudding impact, which must have been my head, as I later determined from the massive crater in the back of my expensive race helmet. I'm bounced up again, my body whomped to the ground, hip bone first, and that jutting, vulnerable bone feels like it's become a bag of dust. And then skipping back up, finally rolling to a stop. I was screaming muffled screams inside my helmet as pain rushed around my body. You always hear that this is when the endorphins kick in, people not even aware they're hurt, but I felt vivid, terrible pain.

Zeitgeist, the rider who'd pulled out in front of me, came running up. I tasted blood in my mouth and tried to sit up. The bike had turned end over end twice, miraculously not hitting me in the process, and bits of plastic fairing, foot pegs, a brake lever, and other Ninja shrapnel littered the sandy ditch. There was gas and oil everywhere. I was disappointed and angry. I couldn't believe I'd crashed after all the work of preparing. I kept thinking, *My bike, my bike.* But then I felt like I was going to vomit and said, "Could you take my helmet off me?" Zeitgeist seemed worried and was convinced I should stay still and leave the helmet on. I tried to take the helmet off myself, but the desire to faint was overriding the desire to puke. I woke with the rider we called Doc holding me up, my helmet off.

Doc was actually a doctor. He had a family practice in I think South San Francisco, but later I heard he became a prison doctor at Folsom. Doc carried a black medical bag stuffed with pills and exuded two opposing but equally creepy qualities: he was always suspiciously sedate, with heavy eyelids and a gentle, almost half-conscious giggle, and he rode with infamous aggression. People knew not to try to pass him because he'd cut them off, take up the whole road. Despite these quirks, I was comforted a real doctor was there. I told Doc my ankle hurt. He pulled my boot off. My foot was ballooning. Doc yelled to Wade to throw him a roll of duct tape, and he then began wrapping tape around my foot, over the sock, tightly. He shoved my foot back into my boot, and as I yelped in pain he said, "Don't take that boot off. You won't be able to get it back on."

Just then a Mexican ambulance came wailing toward us and launched off the road into the ditch, running over and pulverizing all the expensive fiberglass bodywork that had come off my Ninja. Doc and Wade hurriedly lifted me under the armpits, and Doc called to the men getting out of the ambulance, which looked like a 1960s Boy Scout van with a red cross painted on its side, "She's fine. Everything is just fine. No ambulance." Baja medical clinics were rumored to be an expensive scam. I don't know whether this is or was ever true, but Doc and Wade believed it. The two of them carried me across the road to an old hotel that was right there on the highway.

As they laid me down on the steps, I heard Doc, in his half-sedated voice, mumble, "Oh gee, gosh, that's just a shame." I looked across the road and saw my busted-up Kawasaki Ninja strapped into the back of a pickup truck. The truck turned onto the highway and accelerated north. My motorcycle had been stolen, and there was nothing I could do.

As it turned out, race favorite Wade Boyd's motor had blown up. Doc, seeing him on the side of the road and also struggling with mechanical trouble, had pulled over hoping Wade could help him. The third motorcyclist, the guy with the Zeitgeist leathers who had pulled out in front of me, had stopped to say hello. Zeitgeist, after getting them stoned and more or less causing my crash, left. Doc had a leaky exhaust gasket, nothing Wade could fix without a new gasket. After surmising that I was basically okay, Doc started his bike, which sounded terrible: weak and sputtering. Wade laughed and said, "You're going to ride that thing all the way to Cabo?" Doc nodded. "It's better than waiting for the crash truck. You guys will be here all day." He asked again if I wanted any painkillers from his black medical bag (I declined) and took off, his motorcycle wheezing down the road like a sick animal.

Doc was right. Wade and I waited all day. When the crash truck finally showed up, it was after midnight. There were empty beer cans rolling around in the back of the truck with everyone's travel bags and tools, and Reggae on the River and the two crash truck girls seemed to be having a jolly old time. I told them about the theft of my motorcycle and got a consoling "Dude, no fucking way!" from Reggae on the River, who despite his drunkenness recognized my heartache. After Wade's motorcycle was loaded onto the trailer of the truck, Reggae and the crash truck girls decided to eat in the hotel restaurant before heading south. I hurt all over and was exhausted, and with what felt like a broken ankle, but I was too weak to protest.

After plates of food and many more beers were consumed at this old hotel, we finally got on the road. I fell asleep under a blanket in the back of the pickup truck. Around four a.m., I woke up at a gas station near Loreto to the voice of Reggae on the River. "Oh, fuck. Dude. No way!" He held up an empty duffel bag that belonged to one of the racers, the entire bottom of it burned away from road friction. Reggae and the two girls had repacked everybody's stuff after loading Wade's bike in Guerrero Negro, and they had not bothered to secure many of the bags. The bag he held up had been carelessly looped to the tailgate, and as things shifted, it dragged, while many of the other bags rolled out and scattered along the highway between Guerrero Negro and Loreto. My own bag, which contained all of my clothes, my camera, my house keys, all of my identification, and the majority of my money, was gone.

We pulled into Cabo San Lucas just before noon the next day. The bikes were lined up outside the touristy victory restaurant, the Giggling Marlin. Everybody greeted us in their shorts and Cabo 1000 T-shirts. Wade's girlfriend had flown down to meet him, and she came running out of the Marlin with cold and salted margaritas for us. With Wade broken down and out of the running for first place, tall and blond Randy Bradescu, who owned a Marin County motorcycle shop, had won the race. Lee Jones had come in second. My boyfriend had come in near the tail end of the main pack. He said the meal he had eaten at Denny's the night before had made him ill, and that although in the morning he'd been in first place, he'd had to pull over and puke every few miles all the way down to Cabo. As I later saw, this was a pattern with that boyfriend: there were always rancid meals, needy women, nonsensical rules, and jealous, less capable men thwarting him. In light of my own crash, his problems began to seem farcical to me.

Stories were told as pitchers of margaritas went around. My friend Michelle, to the surprise and irritation of many of the guys, had finished in a more-than-respectable sixth place. Stackmaster came in right after Michelle, although his head gasket had leaked all the way down, and he had to keep stopping and applying more sealant. By the time he got to Cabo, his engine was completely covered in orange sealant goop. Sweet Sean Crane in his skeleton-print race leathers had wheelied through the series of toll plazas between Tijuana and Ensenada, in a flagrant refusal to pay what amounted to something like three dollars and fifty cents. He set off an entire convoy of federales, who mistakenly detained my friend James. Eventually they let James go, after ticketing him for clocking 120 in a 50 mph zone. I listened to the stories, finished half my margarita, and limped to the hotel next door to pass out. It was three in the afternoon, and I'd been up for forty-eight hours. When I unzipped my leathers, I saw that the insides of my legs were dark as a blackboard, my entire side around the impacted hip bone was a deep pomegranate red, and I had road rash all over my arms from where my leathers, which were a size too large, had abraded when I hit the ground. I took off my boots but left Doc's duct-tape wrap over my sock.

For the next two days I could barely walk because of my ankle, the bruises darkened and spread, and I woke up periodically with my lake-size scabs attached to the hotel bedsheets. I had my ankle X-rayed and it turned out to be only a severe sprain. My boyfriend paid for the room, since all my money was gone, and he helped me get around, since I could not walk on my own. I think he was proud, as the lore was starting to spread that I'd crashed at 130 mph, with Doc and Wade watching on the roadside. A spectacular bang-up, and it hadn't really been my fault. But ironically, something about crashing made me feel no longer in need of this boyfriend and his domineering nature. I'd suffered without him, and endured. So many bad things had happened—the crash, and then my bike getting stolen—but I felt strangely happy. I hadn't been seriously hurt, and my attitude was intact. I was laughing things off.

The group of well-maintained girlfriends who had flown down to meet their boyfriends in Cabo lent me clean clothes, a bathing suit, shampoo, and sandals, since all my stuff had bumped out of the truck bed as Reggae and the girls partied in the cab. On Lee Jones's advice, I went to the American consulate in Cabo to try to track down my motorcycle. Apparently it was common that when foreigners had accidents, their vehicles were taken to a junkyard north of Guerrero Negro, at which point they became the private property of the family that ran the yard. I got the feeling the family had contacts who lurked at treacherous points on Highway 1, such as the unmarked left-hand turn where I bit it. My bike was taken so fast, no more than thirty minutes after the crash, just calmly wheeled up into a flatbed and strapped down. Through a series of lengthy phone calls, a woman at the consulate located it. She said, "Here is the address, but it's up to you to get it back. They will expect cash."

After two days of Cabo we'd all had enough. Randy Bradescu, who'd won the race, flew from Cabo to another race in Florida and left me his motorcycle to ride up to where mine was supposedly stored. His bike was a BMW K100, sometimes referred to as a Flying Brick for its hefty and square engine. It was huge and top-heavy and difficult for me to steer, but I managed. Heading north up Highway 1, our large group of riders all stopped to spend the night in Mulegé, a beautiful place for luxuriating, with a blue-green bay, white sand beach, and the slow-moving Mulegé River, along which shady date palms grew. I swam in the ocean there, and my road rash loosened into oozing greenish-yellow streamers that sloughed off and trailed around me like seaweed.

Leaving the hotel room the next morning, I noticed a giant tarantula on the door. There were also scorpions in Mulegé. At breakfast, a guy on the ride who'd been a Green Tortoise bus driver, and had taken busloads of people up and down the Baja Peninsula for twenty years, let a scorpion crawl up his arm. We all waited breathlessly, until he flicked it from his wrist to the floor and crushed it with a boot.

We headed north to the junkyard, our group, always up for a new challenge, eager to see if my bike was retrievable. We got to the fenced lot of the junkyard just before dark. I knocked on the door of the house adjacent, while my boyfriend and Stackmaster sneaked into the yard to make sure my bike was there. Wade came in with me for support, while Stack and my boyfriend began wheeling the Ninja out. In poor Spanish I managed to buy my own motorcycle back for 150 dollars that I borrowed from my riding partners.

Every possible thing that could be broken off it in the wreck had been. In the darkening twilight, Stack poached a car headlight out of the lot and affixed it where mine had been, duct-taping it in place. My boyfriend rebent, kicked, and straightened the frame and handlebars until the bike was almost rideable. Stack jammed flathead screwdrivers into the engine scuff plate to serve as foot pegs. My boyfriend started the bike by hot-wiring it (the key had been broken off in the starter when I crashed).

Secretly, I didn't want to ride that motorcycle. It was a mess—the frame was bent, the steering was out of whack, the gas tank was pummeled and cratered, the exhaust canister was ripped wide open (which I tried to fix the next morning by wrapping a cut-open Coke can around it with safety wire). But my boyfriend was pushing for me to ride the crashed bike, and the alternative was Randy's BMW, which was too tall for me and difficult to handle. I left Randy's BMW for the crash truck to pick up and got on my Ninja—the thing that had hurled me onto the ground at 130 miles an hour and then flipped end over end over end.

We set out in the dark, me on the Ninja. The road to Bahia de Los Angeles, where we were planning to spend the night, was in horrible shape. There were grooves worn in the pavement that were exactly the width of my front tire, and when the tire fell into one, my wheel became stuck like a gutter ball, making the bike impossible to control.

In many places the road was washed out completely and was all sand. Long stretches of it were flooded with water. My new nonadjustable, duct-taped car headlight petered out uselessly into the dark and off to the left, rather than illuminating the road down in front of me. I could barely see where I was going, and the bike, with its exhaust pipe ripped open, was as loud as a funny car at the drag strip.

The water in Bahia de Los Angeles is a stunning and artificial chalk blue. Upon waking the next morning, I went for a swim. When I got out of the water, I noticed the pooled blood in the bruises on my legs was starting to drain toward my ankles, leaving long purple streaks running down my legs. That's when the itching began, and didn't cease until two weeks later.

Just north of Bahia de Los Angeles was a dry lakebed that everyone had been excited to visit. Leaving Bahia, we took a sand trail to the lakebed, which meant tricky off-roading on a street bike. The lakebed was a vast, cracked skin of powdery red dust that went for miles in every direction. Everyone was zooming around as fast as they could go, getting sideways on that strange surface. There was no traction, but the lakebed was forgivingly soft, so people were taking chances. I'd had enough adventures and sat and watched with the girlfriends who had flown to Cabo and were riding up as passengers. Stackmaster raced in a circle until he crashed and then stood up laughing, he and his greasy bike, the engine still gooped with sealant, coated in lake dust.

From there, the trip north was long and exhausting. I couldn't keep up with my boyfriend, who didn't want to have to slow down, so I ended up riding with Wade, his girlfriend, and a couple of other friends. About two hundred miles from the border, at a village called San Quintin, we all stopped to get gas, and my companions decided to eat dinner. I kept going by myself. It was nearing dusk, and I was worried about riding in the dark with such a sketchy headlight setup. Night had fallen when I hit the mountains near Ensenada, and I had to keep stopping and retaping the headlight to try to get it to aim at the road. I could barely see. The steering was bent and difficult to control. As huge trucks passed me, they kicked up gravel, which sprayed my tender bruises and pitted my face shield, since my wind fairing was gone, destroyed in the crash.

I stopped at Rosarito to warm up. I went into an American-style diner and ordered hot coffee. My hands were shaking from cold. I was the only person in the place, and the old guy behind the counter set a plate of french fries in front of me that I hadn't ordered but ate gratefully.

A couple of hours after that, I reached the Motel 6 in San Ysidro. I killed the engine, removed my helmet and gloves, and, though I'm ashamed to admit it, I started to cry. They were tears of relief. It was over. I'd made it back in one piece.

Spanning the length of the Baja Peninsula in a single day is like spanning the entire length of the state of California in a day, or driving from San Francisco to Denver, Colorado, in one day. There is that much distance and that much geographical change.

I'm not sure who thought up the concept of the Cabo 1000—I think it may have been Lee and Wade who started it, but I don't know. I picture a few guys sitting around a bar, or at someone's house, the requisite drinking of beer and firing of joints, and somebody mentions the idea of this ride as a sort of outlandish dare. They've all ridden motorcycles around Baja, but the one-day thing is novel. The first race is a success for some, like Wade, who are experienced racers and street riders. It's a disaster for others, who are not, and who either break down, as the stress on the motor and the overall bike is extreme, or crash early on, with no sense of what the dangers are and how to pace themselves on the turny, treacherous roads. This disparity of success and failure is a main point of the event.

The next year, after the inaugural race, more people have heard about the Cabo 1000 and want to try to do it. The goal for most is not to win, but merely to complete the ride without dying. It's a test of will and courage and endurance. When Sean Crane's dicing incident with another rider results in the other guy losing his leg, the ride takes on more mythical proportions. The lost leg becomes a cautionary tale: *It happened to him, don't let it happen to you*, and a sacrifice of sorts: *him, not you*. By losing his leg, that rider becomes an Other, a Not Us. And it's true that there aren't more lost legs. But a detail of that story lingers, an invisible threat that hovers over the event: if you're hurt, you might be on your own. Sean deserted, left the other rider alone with his broken body.

Randy Bradescu, who won the year I rode, and whose bike I'd ridden halfway north, died while competing in the Cabo race four years later. He was winning, out in front of all the other riders, before he took a fatal spill. A few people pulled over to check on him. But once they determined that Randy was dead, they got on their bikes and continued down the peninsula to Cabo and to the after-party and the tour home, Mulegé and dry lakebed included. Randy lay dead, alone on the side of the road. His wife had to send her brother down to get the body, go through skeins of red tape to have it released and sent back to the United States. Randy's wallet had been stolen off his corpse, and with it went his traceable identity, since no friends had been there to tell the Mexican authorities who he was. In the aftermath, someone offered the psychology term "peer apathy."

All of us back in San Francisco from the Cabo race, Michelle, Randy Bradescu, and I met on a Sunday night at Nightbreak, a bar on Haight Street that was a regular hangout spot. I'd previously lived down the street from Nightbreak, and I grew up in walking distance. Randy had just returned from the race in Florida. The three of us were having something of a Cabo reunion. It was Sushi Sunday at Nightbreak, an event hosted by a chef named Nori, a surfer, motorcycle rider, and SF local whom we all adored. We ate sushi and drank beer and acted silly. The DJ played AC/DC and T. Rex, and Randy amused us with dance floor antics that seemed especially funny for a square-looking and extremely tall blond guy in a rugby shirt, given that Nightbreak was an all-black-leather-all-the-time-type biker bar. I was so happy that night. Not risking my life, just having a couple of beers in my hometown, my home scene.

I don't remember if that boyfriend of mine was with us. I broke up with him around then and moved out of the warehouse on Woodward Street. I got my own apartment and started dating someone else, another Moto Guzzi mechanic but a nicer one, my own age and not controlling. The old boyfriend began to appear everywhere I went. I wish there were another term besides "stalking" for what he did, the number of calls he made to my apartment, and his ubiquitous and constant showing up, here and there, everywhere I went, but there isn't. This culminated in him climbing through my apartment window one morning. Luckily my roommate came home and scared him off. I never saw him again, but for a decade I felt hunted.

The person who had originally introduced us, Lawrence Gill, a well-liked machinist who owned a Vincent Black Shadow, the same rare bike my father owns, wrote me a letter apologizing for having been the one to introduce me to that boyfriend. Whom I dated was no one's fault but mine. I was an adult and made my own decisions. I wanted to assure Lawrence Gill of this, but he died before I had the chance. He was killed by a driver who made a left in front of his motorcycle while he was out running an errand. Nori, the friendly sushi chef, whom I'd become closer to after he opened his own restaurant down the block from my new apartment on Pearl Street, died on his motorcycle a few years after that night with Randy and Michelle. Sean Crane died being Sean Crane, late-night riding antics resulting in a fatal crash on Sixteenth Street. Michelle's roommate, a motorcyclist named Julian, died a couple of months after the Cabo race, riding twisty roads up in Marin County. And Randy died four years later, alone, on a Baja roadside, after which the Cabo race was no longer. It ended with Randy's death.

There are two important details about the movie *Girl on a Motorcycle* that I didn't mention earlier. One is that Marianne Faithfull's actual riding scenes, those that aren't her gleefully tossing her head back and clutching the handlebars against an artificial screen, are taken with a stunt double—a huge, hulking man dressed just like her in tight black leather, a blond wig flapping stiffly against his broad shoulders and plastered over his Teutonic forehead, as I discovered by watching the film on slow. The other is the abrupt and lurid final scene: after a desperate visit to a rustic tavern where Marianne Faithfull drinks alone, kirsch after kirsch, brokenhearted over Alain Delon, she gets on her motorcycle, and things start to get weird. She writhes in the seat as if making love to the bike and starts swerving recklessly, splitting lanes on the autobahn. She loses control and slams broadside into a truck, is launched up over the cab, and plows forcefully through the windshield of a four-door sedan. She dies, the lower half of her leather-clad body jutting from the front of the car. That's the end of the film.

I fixed up and sold my Ninja for good money after returning from Cabo. I remember wanting to ask the guy who bought it not to ride it. I remember thinking I was passing along a death machine. But I was young and broke. I took the money and said nothing but "have fun." I didn't tell him to be safe. And I didn't tell him the Ninja had a stolen engine. I'd blown up the original engine on a solo trip to Boise, Idaho, a year or so before the Cabo race. My then boyfriend had procured me another motor. I didn't know, initially, that it was stolen, but I eventually learned it had come from a guy named Tiny, an enormous teenager who, we all knew, lifted locked, parked motorcycles single-handedly into his flatbed truck, high on crystal meth and PCP. And the truth is, mine was not the first hot engine that passed through our warehouse on Woodward, its serial numbers restamped, involving a skillful fracturing of the crystal structure under the numbers, which can normally be traced by X-ray. When I sold the Ninja, I was confident the guy who bought it would have no problem getting it registered, because its frame and engine numbers matched.

I bought another bike after that, a Cagiva Elefant 650, but I didn't ride it much, and eventually sold that too. Thereafter my motorcycle hobby consisted of my father and me tinkering with the Vincent Black Shadow every few years. I used to jauntily ride it around San Francisco for show, and took it to British bike expos. Spent a lot of time trying to track down rare replacement parts. But it's been a long while since we gave it any attention. It could use starting, at the very least.

WE ARE ORPHANS HERE

Standing on a corner in Shuafat Refugee Camp in East Jerusalem, I watched as a boy, sunk down behind the steering wheel of a beat-up sedan, zoomed through an intersection with his arm out the driver's-side window, signaling like a NASCAR racer pulling in for a pit stop. I was amazed. He looked about twelve.

"No one cares here," my host, Baha Nababta, said, laughing at my astonishment. "Anyone can do anything they want."

As Baha and I walked around Shuafat, teenagers fell in behind us, forming a kind of retinue. Among them were cool kids who looked like cool kids the world over, tuned in to that teenage frequency, a dog whistle with global reach. I noticed that white was a popular color. White, slouchy, pegged jeans, white polo shirts, white high-tops. Maybe white has extra status in a place where many roads are unpaved and turn to mud, where garbage is everywhere, literally, and where water shortages make it exceedingly difficult to keep people and clothing clean.

So few nonresidents enter Shuafat that my appearance there seemed to be a highly unusual event, met with warm greetings verging on hysteria, crowds of kids following along. "Hello, America!" they called excitedly. I was a novelty, but also, I was with Baha Nababta, a twenty-nine-year-old Palestinian community organizer beloved by the kids of Shuafat. Those who followed us wanted not just my attention but his. Baha had a rare kind of charisma. Camp-counselor charisma, you might call it. He was a natural leader of boys. Every kid we passed knew him and either waved or stopped to speak to him. Baha founded a community center so that older children would have a place to hang out, because there is no open space in Shuafat Refugee Camp, no park, not a single playground, nowhere for kids to go, not even a street, really, where they can play, because there are no sidewalks, most of the narrow roads barely fitting the cars that ramble down them. Younger kids tapped me on the arms and wanted to show me the mural they painted with Baha. The road they helped to pave with Baha, who supervised its completion. The plants they planted with Baha along a narrow strip. Baha, Baha, Baha.

It was like that with the adults too. They all wanted his attention. His phone was blowing up in his pocket as we walked. He finally answered. There was a dispute between a man whose baby died at a clinic and the doctor who treated the baby. The man whose baby died tried to burn the doctor alive, and now the doctor was in critical condition in a hospital in Jerusalem. Throughout the two days I spent with Baha, I heard more stories like this that he was asked to help resolve. People relied on him. He had a vision for the Shuafat camp, where he was born and raised, that went beyond what could be imagined from within the very limited confines of the place.

In an area of high-rise apartment buildings clustered around a mosque with spindly, futuristic minarets, a pudgy boy of ten or eleven called over to us. "My dad is trying to reach you," he said to Baha. Baha told me that the buildings in that part of the camp had no water and that everyone was contacting him about it. He had not been answering his phone, he confessed, because he didn't have any good news yet for the residents. I got the impression Baha was something like an informal mayor, on whom people depended to resolve disputes, build roads, put together volunteer committees, and try to make Shuafat camp safe for children.

The building next to us was twelve stories. Next to it was another twelve-story building. High-rise apartments in the camp are built so close together that if a fire should happen, the results would be devastating. There would be no way to put it out. The buildings are all built of stone blocks that feature, between blocks, wooden wedges that stick out intermittently, as if the builders never returned to fill the gaps with mortar. I gazed up at a towering facade, with its strange wooden wedges, which made the building look like a model of a structure, except that it was occupied. The pudgy boy turned to me as I craned my neck. "This building is stupidly built," he said. "It's junk."

"Do you live here?" I asked him, and he said yes.

Shuafat Refugee Camp is inside Jerusalem proper, according to the municipal boundaries that Israel declared after the Six-Day War in 1967. (Though the entire walled area is frequently referred to as the Shuafat Refugee Camp, the actual camp, run by the United Nations' relief agency for Palestinian refugees, is only a small portion. Adjacent to the camp are three neighborhoods that are the responsibility of the city of Jerusalem.) The Palestinian Authority has no jurisdiction there: the camp is, according to Israeli law, inside Israel, and the people who live there are Jerusalem residents, but they are refugees in their own city. Residents pay taxes to Israel, but the camp is barely serviced. There is very little legally supplied water, a scarcely functioning sewage system, essentially no garbage pickup, no road building, no mail service (the streets don't even have names, much less addresses), virtually no infrastructure of any kind. There is no adequate school system. Israeli emergency fire and medical services do not enter the camp. The Israeli police enter only to make arrests; they provide no security for camp residents. There is chaotic land registration. While no one knows how many people really live in the Shuafat camp and its three surrounding neighborhoods, which is roughly one square kilometer, it's estimated that the population is around eighty thousand. They live surrounded by a twenty-five-foot concrete wall, a wall interspersed with guard towers and trapdoors that swing open when Israeli forces raid the camp, with reinforcements in the hundreds or even, as in December 2015, more than a thousand troops.

Effectively, there are no laws in the Shuafat Refugee Camp, despite its geographical location inside Jerusalem. The Shuafat camp's original citizens were moved from the Old City, where they sought asylum in 1948 during the Arab-Israeli War, to the camp's boundaries starting in 1965, when the camp was under the control of the Jordanian government, with more arriving, in need of asylum, during and after the war in 1967. Now, fifty years after Israel's 1967 boundaries were drawn, even Israeli security experts don't quite know why the Shuafat Refugee Camp was placed inside the Jerusalem municipal boundaries. The population was much smaller then and surrounded by beautiful green, open forest, which stretched to the land on which the Jewish settlement of Pisgat Ze'ev was later built. (The forest is still there, visible beyond the separation wall but inaccessible to camp residents on account of the wall.) Perhaps the Israelis were hoping the camp's residents could be relocated, because they numbered only a few thousand. Instead, the population of the camp exploded in the following decades into the tens of thousands. In 1980, Israel passed a law declaring Jerusalem the "complete and united" capital of Israel. In 2004, Israel began erecting the concrete wall around the camp, cutting inside Israel's own declared boundaries, as if to stanch and cauterize the camp from "united" Jerusalem.

If high-rise buildings are not typically conjured by the term "refugee camp," neither is an indoor shopping mall, but there is one in the Shuafat camp: two floors and a third that was under construction when I visited, an escalator up and down, and a store called Fendi, which sells inexpensive women's clothes. The mall owner greeted us with exuberance and pulled Baha aside to ask for advice of some kind. A teenager who worked at a mall ice-cream parlor, a hipster in a hoodie and eyeglass frames without lenses, did a world-class beatbox for me and Moriel Rothman-Zecher, a writer and organizer who had walked me into the camp in order to make introductions between Baha and me and to serve as my Arabic interpreter. Moriel and the teenager from the ice-cream shop took turns. Moriel's own beatbox was good but not quite up to the Shuafat Refugee Camp beatbox standards. We met an accountant named Fahed, who had just opened his shop in the mall to prepare taxes for residents. He was stunned to hear English being spoken and eager to use his own. The tax forms are in Hebrew, he explained, so most people in the camp must hire a bilingual accountant to complete them.

Before the separation wall was constructed, the mall was bulldozed twice by the Israeli authorities, but the owner rebuilt both times. Since the wall has gone up, the Israelis have not tried to demolish any large buildings in Shuafat, though they have destroyed individual homes. Armed Palestinian gangsters could take away someone's land or apartment at any moment. A fire or earthquake would be catastrophic. There are multiple risks to buying property in the Shuafat camp, but the cost of an apartment there can be less than a tenth of what an apartment would cost on the other side of the separation wall in East Jerusalem. And living in Shuafat is a way to try to hold on to Jerusalem residency status. Jerusalem residents have a coveted blue ID card, meaning they can enter Israel in order to work and support their families, unlike Palestinians with green, or West Bank, ID cards, who need many supporting documents in order to enter Israel—to work or for any other reason—and who also must pass through military checkpoints like Qalandiya, which can require waiting in hours-long lines. Jerusalem residency is, quite simply, a lifeline to employment, a matter of survival.

There are also non-Jerusalemites in the camp. Since the wall went up, it has become a sanctuary, a haven. I met people from Gaza, who cannot leave the square kilometer of the camp or they risk arrest, because it is illegal for Gazans to enter Israel or the occupied West Bank except with Israeli permission, which is almost never granted. I met a family of Brazilian Palestinians with long-expired passports who also cannot leave the camp, because they do not have West Bank green IDs or Jerusalem blue IDs.

Shuafat camp is often depicted in the international media as the most dangerous place in Jerusalem, a crucible of crime, jihad, and trash fires. On the day I arrived, garbage was indeed smoldering in great heaps just inside the checkpoint entrance, against the concrete separation wall, flames jumping thinly in the strong morning sun. I had been to countries that burn their trash; it is a smell you get used to. My main concern, over the weekend I spent in the camp, was not getting my foot run over by a car. If you are seriously hurt in the camp, there isn't much help. Ill or injured people are carried through the checkpoint, on foot or by car, and put in ambulances on the other side of the wall. According to residents of the camp, several people have unnecessarily died in this manner.

As we walked, I began to understand how to face the traffic without flinching, to expect that drivers are experienced at navigating such incredible human density. I asked Baha if people were ever run over by cars, assuming he would say no.

"Yes, all the time," he said. "A child was just killed this way," he added. I hugged the walls of the apartment buildings as we strolled. Later that evening, I watched as a tiny boy riding a grown man's bicycle was bumped by a car. He crashed in the road. I ran to help him. He was crying, holding out his abraded hands. I remembered how painful it is to scrape your palms, how many nerve endings there are. A Palestinian man told the little boy he was okay and ruffled his hair.

When I asked Baha if garbage was burned by the separation wall because it was safer—a way to contain a fire, like a giant fireplace—he shook his head. "It's, aah, symbolic." In other words, garbage is burned by the wall because the wall is Israeli. Drugs are sold along the wall by the Israeli checkpoint, not for symbolic reasons. The camp organizers, like Baha, cannot effectively control the drug trade in a zone patrolled by the Israeli police and monitored by security cameras. Dealers are safe there from the means of popular justice exacted inside the camp. The most heavily militarized area of the camp is perhaps its most lawless.

The popular drug the dealers sell is called Mr. Nice Guy, which is sometimes categorized as a "synthetic cannabinoid"—a meaningless nomenclature. It is highly toxic, and its effects are nothing like cannabis. It can bring on psychosis. It damages brains and ruins lives. Baha told me that Mr. Nice Guy is popular with kids as young as eight. Empty packets of it sifted around at our feet as we crossed the large parking lot where buses pick up six thousand children daily and transport them through the checkpoint for school, because the camp has only one public school, for elementary students. Every afternoon, children stream back into camp, passing the dealers and users who cluster near the checkpoint.

I didn't see the dealers, but I doubt Baha would have pointed them out. What I mostly noticed were children working, being industrious, trying to find productive ways to live in a miserable environment and to survive. Across from Baha's house, a group of kids ran a car wash. We waved to them from Baha's roof. Baha introduced me to a group of teenage boys who owned their own moped-and-scooter-repair service. He took me to a barbershop where kids in flawless outfits with high side fades were hanging out, listening to music, while a boy of about thirteen gave a haircut to a boy of about five. A young teenager in a pristine white polo shirt and delicate gold neck chain flexed his baby potato of a biceps and announced his family name: "Alqam!"

The children in the barbershop were all Alqam. They ran the shop. They were ecstatic to see Baha. We were all ecstatic. The language barrier between the boys and me only thickened our collective joy, as my interpreter Moriel was whisked into a barber chair for a playfully coerced beard trim, on the house. The boys and I shouldered up for selfies, put on our sunglasses, and posed. Whenever men shook my hand after Baha introduced me, I sensed—especially after Moriel left that afternoon—that men and boys would not get so physically close to a Palestinian woman who was a stranger. But I was an American woman, and I was with Baha, which made me something like an honorary man.

Later I told myself and everyone else how wonderful it was in the Shuafat camp. How safe I felt. How positive Baha was. All of that still feels true. But I also insisted, to myself and everyone else, that Baha never expressed any fears for his own safety. In looking at my notes, I see now that my insistence on this point was sheer will. A fiction. It's right there in the notes. He said he was nervous. He said he'd been threatened.

Also in my notes, this:

Baha says, two types
   1. Those who want to help make a better life
   2. Those who want to destroy everything
And in parentheses I'd written: *Arms trade. Drugs trade. Construction profits. No oversight wanted.*

"I wanted you to meet the boys because they are nice people," Baha said, after we left the barbershop. "But they do all carry guns." It was only after I returned home to the United States that I learned, in the banal and cowardly way, with a few taps on my computer, that two Alqam boys, cousins who were twelve and fourteen, had been accused of stabbing, with a knife and scissors, an Israeli security guard on a tram in East Jerusalem. I still don't know whether they were related to the boys in the barbershop. Several of the young assailants in what has been called the Knife Intifada have been from the Shuafat camp, which has also been the site of huge and violent protests in which Palestinians have been killed by Israeli forces. In 2015, three children from the Shuafat Refugee Camp lost eyes from sponge bullets shot by Israeli forces.

The other thing I suppressed, besides Baha's admissions of fear, was his desire for police. I didn't write that down. It wasn't part of my hero narrative, because the police are not part of my hero narrative. "Even if they have to bring them from India," he said several times, "we need police here. We cannot handle the disputes on our own. People take revenge. They murder."

*   *   *

A Middle East correspondent I met in the West Bank, hearing that I was going to spend the weekend in the Shuafat camp, asked me if I "planned to visit Shit Lake" while there. Apparently that was his single image of the place. I assumed he was referring to a sewage dump, but Baha never mentioned it, and after seeing Baha's pleasure in showing me the community center, the roads his committee had built, the mall, which was the only open gathering space, all things that, for him, were hopeful, I wasn't going to ask him for Shit Lake.

That correspondent had never set foot in the camp. I hadn't expected to either, until I was invited on an extensive tour of the occupied West Bank, including East Jerusalem, and was asked to choose a subject to write about for an anthology on the Israeli occupation of Palestine. With no previous experience in the region, and little knowledge, I gravitated instinctually to Shuafat camp. From my own time there, the sustaining image is shimmering white. The kids, dressed in white. The buildings, a baked tone of dusty, smoke-stained white. The minarets, all white. And there was the 1972 Volkswagen Beetle in gleaming white, meticulously restored. It was on the shop floor of a garage run by Baha's friend Adel. A classic-car enthusiast and owner myself, I wanted to talk to Adel about the car. He showed me his garage, his compressor, his lift. Like the escalator in the mall, these were things you would never expect to find in a place without services.

We sat, and Adel made coffee. He and Baha told me about the troubles with the drug Mr. Nice Guy. They said every family has an addict among its children and sometimes among the older people as well. A third of the population is strung out on it, they said. It makes people crazy, Adel and Baha agreed. Was there a link, I asked, between Mr. Nice Guy and the kids who decided, essentially, to end it all by running at an Israeli soldier with a knife? They each concurred that there was. Two years earlier, Baha said, by way of contrast, there was a man from the Shuafat camp who did a deadly car ramming. The Israelis came and blew up his house. He was older, Baha said, and out of work, and he decided that he was finally ready to lose everything. With the kids, Baha said, it's different. It's an act of impulsive courage. The drug helps enormously with that.

Adel kept making reference to his nine-year-old daughter, who is physically disabled and cannot attend school. I asked to meet her or Adel asked if I wanted to meet her. Either way we ended up in Adel's large apartment, and his daughter Mira was wheeled out to the living room. Mira was burned over most of her body and is missing part of one arm and a kneecap. Her face and scalp are disfigured. A school bus filled with children from the Shuafat camp were on a trip to Ramallah when their bus collided with a truck on wet roads. The bus overturned and burst into flames. Five children and a teacher burned to death. Dozens were injured. Emergency services were delayed by confusion over who had jurisdiction. As a result, Mira and other children had to be taken in the cars of bystanders to the closest hospital. The accident took place between the Adam settlement and Qalandiya checkpoints, in what is called Area C of the West Bank, which is entirely under Israeli control. The likelihood of something like this occurring was well-known. Later, a report from Ir Amim, an Israeli human-rights group, established that the tragedy resulted from the multiple challenges of living beyond the separation barrier. Roads were substandard. There were too many children on the bus, the children had no access to education in their own communities, and there was no oversight.

"When the accident happened, we didn't know how to cope with it," Baha told me. Someone got up on a loading dock in the camp and called out the names of the dead. Afterward, Baha and Adel cried all the time. They felt that the lives of Shuafat's children were disposable. They decided to start their own volunteer emergency team, through WhatsApp, and it has eighty members, who are trained in first aid and in special skills they are ready to employ at a moment's notice. They are saving up to purchase their own Shuafat camp ambulance, whose volunteer drivers will be trained medical professionals, like Baha's wife, Hiba, who is a nurse.

Baha, I noticed, seemed more optimistic about their emergency team, and about the future, than Adel did. At one point, Adel, who has a shattered and frantic but loving, warm energy, turned to me and said, "We are orphans here."

Mira, who had been transferred from her wheelchair to the couch, sat and fidgeted. She understood no English but was forced to quietly pretend she was listening. I kept smiling at her, and she smiled back. I was desperate to give her something, to promise something. It's very difficult to see a child who has suffered so tremendously. It's basically unbearable. I should give her the ring I was wearing, I thought. But then I saw that it would never fit her fingers, which were very swollen and large, despite her young age; her development, after the fire, was thwarted because her bones could not properly grow. I'd give her my earrings, was my next idea, and then I realized that her ears had been burned off in the fire. I felt obscene. I sat and smiled as if my oversize teeth could beam a protective fiction over this poor child, blind us both to the truth, that no shallow gesture or petty generosity would make any lasting difference, and that her life was going to be difficult.

The travel agency in the Shuafat mall is called Hope. There is a toy store in the mall called the Happy Child. The children I met were all

Baha's kids, part of his group, on his team, drafting off his energy, which was relentlessly upbeat.

I have to re-create, with all the precision I can manage, to remember what I am able to, about Baha. I see Baha in his pink polo shirt, tall and handsome, but with a soft belly that somehow reinforces his integrity, makes him imperfectly, perfectly human. Baha singing "Bella Ciao" in well-keyed Italian, a language he learned at nineteen, on the trip that changed his life, working with Vento di Terra, a community-development and human-rights group based in Italy. Later, I sent a video of Baha singing to various Italian friends, leftists who were thrilled that a guy in a Palestinian refugee camp knew the words to "Bella Ciao."

Baha's friends and relatives all hugging me and cheek-kissing me, the women bringing out boxes that contained their hand-embroidered wedding dresses, insisting I try on each dress, whose colors and designs specified where they were from: one in black with white stitching, from Ramallah. Cream with red, Jerusalem. We took photos, laughing, of me in each dress, with the woman it belonged to on my arm.

Everyone imploring me to come back, and to bring Remy, my eight-year-old, and I was sure that I would come back, and bring Remy, because I had fallen in love with these people.

And in the background of the hugs and kisses, in almost every home where we spent time, the TV playing the Islamic channel, Palestine Al-Yawm, a relentless montage of blood, smoke, fire, and kaffiyeh-wrapped fighters with M16s.

The constant hospitality. Coffee, tea, mint lemonade, ice water, all the drinks I politely accepted. Drank and then sloshed along, past faded wheat-pasted posters of jihadist martyrs.

Late at night, Baha and Hiba decided to show me their digital wedding photo book. It was midnight, their two young daughters asleep on couches around us. Hiba propped an iPad on a table—she was four months pregnant, expecting her third child, a boy—and we looked at every last image, hundreds of images, of her and Baha in highly curated poses and stiff wedding clothes, her fake-pearl-and-rhinestone tiara, her beautiful face neutralized by heavy makeup, but the makeup is part of the ritual, and the ritual is part of the glory. The two of them in a lush park in West Jerusalem. Every picture we looked at was, for them watching me see the images, a new delight: there were more and more and more. For me, they all started to run together; it was now one in the morning, I was exhausted, but I made myself regard each photograph as something unique, a vital integer in the stream of these people's refusal to be reduced.

I slept in what they called their Arabic room, on low cushions, a barred window above me issuing a cool breeze. I listened to roosters crow and the semiautomatic weapons being fired at a nearby wedding celebration, and eventually I drifted into a calm and heavy sleep.

The next day, Baha had meetings to attend to try to solve the water problem. I spoke to Hiba about their kids. She asked me at what age Remy started his piano lessons. "I want music lessons for the girls," she said. "I think it's very good for their development." As she said it, more machine-gun fire erupted from the roof of a nearby building. "I want them to know the feel, the smells, of a different environment. To be able to imagine other lives."

When I think of Hiba Nababta wanting what I want for my child, her rightful desire that her kids should have an equal chance, everything feels hopeless and more obscene, even, than my wanting to give earrings to a child without ears.

I went with Hiba that morning to her mother's house, where she and Hiba's sisters were preparing an exquisite meal of stuffed grape leaves and stuffed squashes, the grape leaves and vegetables grown on her mother's patio. We were all women, eating together in relaxed company. A sister-in-law came downstairs to join us, sleepy, beautiful, with long red nails and hair dyed honey blond, in her pajamas and slippers. She said that she was leaving for New Jersey with her husband, Hiba's brother, and their new baby. Relatives had arranged for them to immigrate. She would learn English and go to school.

When it was time to say goodbye, a younger sister was appointed to walk me to the checkpoint. Halfway there, I assured her I could walk alone, and we said goodbye. On the main road, shopkeepers came out to wave and smile. Everyone seemed to know who I was: the American who had come to meet with Baha.

At the checkpoint, the Palestinian boy in front of me was detained. I was next, and the soldiers were shocked to see an American, as they would have been shocked to see any non-Palestinian. There was much consternation in the reinforced station. My passport went from hand to hand. The commander approached the scratched window. "You're a Jew, right?" he blurted into the microphone. For the context in which he asked, for its reasoning, I said no. But in fact, I'm ethnically half-Jewish, on my father's side, although I was not raised with any connection to Judaism or Jewish culture. My father's parents identified as "American communists," and they sent Christmas presents every year. My mother is a white Protestant from Tennessee. We do a ham on Easter. I might have said, "I'm technically part-Jewish," but I found the question un-answerable, on account of its conflation of Zionism and Jewish identity. My Yiddish-speaking Odessan great-grandfather was a clothing merchant on Orchard Street in Manhattan's Lower East Side. My grandfather worked in his shop as a boy. That is classically Jewish—as is supplanting Jewish identity for communism—but my sense of self, of what it might mean to inherit some trace of that lineage, was not the kind of patrimony the soldier was asking after. I was eventually waved along.

The day I left Shuafat camp was April 17, 2016. Fifteen days later, on May 2, Baha Nababta was murdered in the camp. An unknown person approached on a motorcycle as Baha worked with roughly a hundred fellow camp residents to pave a road. In front of this very large crowd of people, working together, the person on the motorcycle shot at Baha ten times and fled. Seven bullets hit him.

It is now December. Baha's wife, Hiba, has given birth to their son. His father is gone. His mother is widowed. But a baby—a baby can thrive no matter. A baby won't even know, until it is told, that someone is missing.

EARTH ANGEL

ear Astronaut Selection Officer:

I am a civilian who would like to be considered for the one-year astronaut training program.

I would be most grateful if you would send me information, application forms, and any such material you feel might be helpful in this regard.

Sincerely,
Denis H. Johnson

The writer Denis Johnson sent the above letter on April 15, 1991. A copy of it is among his papers at the Harry Ransom Center, at the University of Texas at Austin. A few years ago, I took a picture of the letter. Recently I sent it to a friend. This friend, a writer who admires and has publicly endorsed Denis Johnson, said to me, "I can't imagine what he was thinking when he wrote this." But I felt I could imagine exactly what he was thinking: He was looking to get off this ball. To travel to outer space. What does it mean to go to outer space? To leave your life, escape the confines of this world, and live to tell.

There are other ways of getting off this ball and I believe that

Denis H. Johnson tried a few. The *H.*, by the way, stands not for "Holy," like between Jesus and Christ, but "Hale," apparently his middle name. You can also call him Commodore. It's what he told me I might call him when I once, long ago, wrote him a slavish letter in which I addressed him as "Mr. Johnson." He wrote back that if I insisted on formality to call him Commodore, which was his rank. I haven't done the biographical work to confirm it, but I don't think he was ever a naval officer or the president of a yacht club. I take it as a joke and also not a joke. Call him Commodore. Elvis is the King, and so why not?

In the spring of 1999, eight years after Denis Johnson wrote to NASA trying to get to outer space, he read at the Dia Center for the Arts in New York City, along with the poet Jean Valentine. The room was packed; there were probably a thousand people there. I had arrived about three hours early for the reading, in order to land a seat (and because I was *that* kind of acolyte). I remember with grainy accuracy the person who was in the neighboring chair: a tall, thin guy about my age in free-box grandpa clothes and horn-rimmed glasses, shakily removing a bottle of Pepto-Bismol from the inside pocket of his coat, and periodically taking swigs. The notes he scribbled during the reading were probably as embarrassing as mine. Luckily mine are lost. I don't need them. I remember the poems that Johnson read, including "Traveling," from his collection *The Veil.* He read "Traveling" three times. The first time, his rhythm was off, so he wanted to try again. The second time, it seemed he wasn't able to recapture the effect of the poem, and so he read it once more. Not for us, the audience, but to try to remember what work he'd originally thought the poem might do, back when he had written it. There is a line in it about the light coming in through a barbershop's windows: "the shifting illumination in the place made it seem we were traveling." The third time he read the poem, he slowed at this line. He'd reconnected.

*   *   *

Denis Johnson understood the impulse to check out. He understood a lot of things, including the contradictory nature of truth. He was the son of a US State Department employee stationed overseas, a well-to-do suburban American boy who was "saved" from the penitentiary, as he put it, by "the Beatnik category." He went to college, published a book of poetry by the age of nineteen (*The Man Among the Seals*), went to graduate school and got an MFA, but was also an alkie drifter and heroin addict: a "real" writer, in other words (who, like any *really* real writer, can't be pigeonholed by one coherent myth or by trite ideas about the school of life). Later he got clean and became some kind of Christian, published many novels and a book of outstanding essays, lived in remote northern Idaho but traveled to and wrote about multiple zones of conflict—Somalia, Liberia, Sierra Leone, Afghanistan, and famously, in *Tree of Smoke*, wartime Vietnam. Perhaps being raised abroad, in various far-flung locations (Germany, the Philippines, and Japan), gave him a better feeling for the lost and ugly American, the juncture of the epic and pathetic, the suicidal tendencies of the everyday joe, which seem to have been his wellspring.

His connection to "people who totaled their souls," as one character puts it in *The Largesse of the Sea Maiden*, his final contribution to literature, is a central tenor of his work. His passion for wrecked people certainly spawned a kind of cult status, which was rampant in the 1990s, when I was young and Johnson came into his phosphorous popularity. It was hero worship of totaled souls, by totaled souls. Hero worship isn't malicious. No harm was meant. And yet it's important not to allow that phase of Johnson's fame to shape the achievements of a writer who was much more serious than a cult phenomenon might ever suggest. I see these distinctions in a way I was unable to twenty years back, because I was caught up in a narrow margin among people who read only a handful of books, and of a certain kind: Nelson Algren's *The Man with the Golden Arm*, *The Basketball Diaries* by Jim Carroll, some Bukowski, some Burroughs, *You Can't Win* by Jack Black, and Johnson's 1992 story collection *Jesus' Son*. We were young bohemians who thought you were supposed to live like that. And we only read people who lived like it. In Iowa City, where I had friends (Iowans, I should clarify, not anyone from the Writers' Workshop), bar talk was all about Denis Johnson and *Jesus' Son*. "He told and retold those stories until his delivery was perfect, and at that point, he wrote them down," a crackhead I knew said to me. I later asked Denis Johnson if this was true of his process: No, it was not true. "I just wrote them the normal way," he said, "one sentence at a time."

Johnson died in 2017 at the age of sixty-seven, which feels tragically premature. His legacy is to have overshot his 1990s cult celebrity by light-years. He outlived all that and in a way never lived it, even as he certainly did, biographically speaking. I suspect that he was only incidentally a user and drinker but deliberately, and fatefully, a serious artist. He is not for hipsters who scribble and crackheads who read. He is not a means to anyone else's identity formation. His ambitions were, in their own way, as broad and burgeoning as Dostoyevsky's. He is a writer for all time.

Also, he's for women, I'll assert, at least in his work, which is the only thing that ultimately matters. Jamie, the female protagonist of *Angels*, his first and in a way his most perfect novel, looks out the window of a bus and imagines "a great blade protruding for miles from her window, leveling the whole suburbs six feet above the ground." Any man who could write that of a woman's fantasies has a pretty good grasp of us. His female characters—like Jamie or the tough and shadowy unnamed woman who narrates *The Stars at Noon*—are as complex and pissed off as the men. (That doesn't mean the female gender or species or whatever that is—whatever I is—doesn't get to also be the object of longing and idealization, doesn't get to have the largesse, let's say, of sea maidens: be women to cry on and hold. It's not one or the other.)

Johnson was an accomplished poet and novelist before he wrote *Jesus' Son*, but that work and *Largesse of the Sea Maiden* mark out the stakes of his literary arc, in part because they are his only two collections of short stories, and for the way they mirror each other and produce, in their differences, a clear artistic direction. The early, densely poetic scenes in *Jesus' Son* have given way, in *Largesse*, to subtler work, which seems no longer about language virtuosity but something attenuated and humble, and even more ambitious.

The recurring character in *Jesus' Son*, sometimes called Fuckhead, had the rhetorical advantage of mysterious hindsight. His was a voice that was able to compress flights of feeling and self-pity and corrosive regret into the eternally quotable:

> "We all believed we were tragic, and we drank."
>
> "We would be put a stop to, and it wouldn't be our fault."
>
> "Sometimes what I wouldn't give to have us sitting in a bar again at 9:00 a.m. telling lies to one another, far from God."
>
> "Where are my women now, with their sweet wet words and ways, and the miraculous balls of hail popping in a green translucence in the yards?"

The "green translucence in the yards" is high-flown, and yet I do not doubt that it was the salient vision to share. Every sentiment and gesture in *Jesus' Son* feels true, and not all writers approach anything true in what they write, but instead have other types of gifts, and skills, for braiding imagery or manipulating cadence, pulling off stunts. Literature, even really good literature, is sometimes more like a beautiful baroque carpet than it is like life. Denis Johnson, in all his work, aimed to locate the hidden, actual face of things. But the new stories build without those miraculous balls of hail, and their truths are deeper, and more precise, true as you would true a wheel. *Jesus' Son*, by comparison, seems like work produced by the forceful energy of all the saved-up characters bursting to be seen and known by those who weren't there, weren't in the bar or out at the farm on the Old Highway. Weren't riding around with Georgie, high on stolen hospital meds. *The Largesse of the Sea Maiden* operates on a different set of registers; it feels like the paced vision of a writer who has been made to understand that life is fairly rude and somewhat short, but the world contains an uneven distribution of grace, and wisdom lies in recognizing where it—such grace—has presented itself. The stories are about death and immortality, art and its reach, and they ask elemental questions about fiction, not as a literary genre but as a human tendency. The characters make narrative from what they witness: such as an Afghanistan war veteran telling a group of friends at a dinner party that he'll remove his prosthetic leg if a woman who is present agrees to kiss his stump; she refuses but later marries this vet. As the narrator says to the reader: "You and I know what goes on." Another man, wandering in his bathrobe in the quiet of night, encounters a sign for a store he believes offers "Sky and Celery," but in fact it says "Ski and Cyclery." "What goes on" is never a given, and always subjective. Wisps of narrativizing in this final collection shape thoughts that are sly, open-ended, and meticulously wise. It could be that the more a person knows, the less he needs to perform his gifts. These stories ask you to step into the room and listen closely. They are not showy anthems, and in many cases, they have dispensed with hindsight altogether.

Mark Cassandra, in "The Starlight on Idaho," is less than a week into rehab and has all the raw fragility of a person newly in recovery. He can't talk to us like Fuckhead did, in other words, even if he's a Fuckhead-type guy, because Fuckhead had that uncanny distance from his own life. Of group therapy, Mark Cassandra says, "It's basically a circle of terrified bullshitters kissing this guy's ass named Jerry." The genius in the sentence is that loose, colloquial construction "kissing this guy's ass named Jerry." The bullshitting is the fiction, but Mark Cassandra is failing at it. He can't even get through a whole cigarette without "thinking crazy." "I know I don't know what's good for me," he says, in perfect counterpoint to Fuckhead's capacity to poetize and reflect. That Johnson returned here to a rehab scene must be acknowledged as a clue, perhaps that he was determined to add to what he'd done before, to get something right or to get it from a different vantage, like his reread, that night at the Dia, of the poem "Traveling," but this time, to use memory and the restraint of later-life maturity to produce a raw immediacy. The character Mark Cassandra is not Fuckhead and neither is he Denis Johnson. Or maybe he is, but without the long view. He's a person in a moment, damaged, addled, and afraid. He's wearing secondhand running shoes and vowing to himself that he's going "to change or die trying."

In another story, "Strangler Bob," we reencounter Dundun, a secondary character from *Jesus' Son*, but at a younger age and through the eyes of a Fuckhead-like character who this time is called Dink. This is the prequel, the primal scene, where a sinister jail-mate known as Strangler Bob announces the fate of Dink, Dundun, and a guy named BD. They will all three end up murderers, Strangler Bob predicts, in a scene that echoes, strikingly, a moment in Johnson's novel *Tree of*

Smoke, when an admiral rolls down the window of his white Ford Galaxie and warns Bill Houston and the unsavory company he's scavenged while on shore leave in Honolulu, "Hard times are coming for assholes like you."

Hard times indeed come for Bill Houston. The first-person narrator of "Strangler Bob" also bears out the ominous prediction that he will kill, even if he does so inadvertently. He picks up some version of terminal sauce, an unnamed disease (probably hepatitis C), and presumes he has shared it with innumerable strangers by selling his blood to buy wine. The emphasis, devastatingly, is not on the narrator, suddenly, but on his impact on other people, and on the question of judgment, a final one.

That's one of the heavier moments. Other stories are infused with a kind of deep-core comedy, a layer of humor inside narratives of doubles, doppelgängers, death, and the question of life after death. The first story, which shares the book's title, is a series of views on life from the perspective of an adman approaching the end of his career, but they mostly involve death. In one scenelet, called "Casanova," the adman encounters someone he takes to be an old colleague but is actually that colleague's look-alike son, who tells the narrator his father is dead. They speak staring at each other in a mirror above the sinks in a men's room (in Trump Tower, of all places). The adman avoids looking down at the other man's trousers and shoes, not wanting to confirm that the doppelgänger of his dead colleague is the same person who has just passed to him, under the bathroom-stall partition, a square of toilet paper with a lewd proposition. In another scene, the adman reflects on an eccentric artist he barely knew who killed himself. He gets a call from an ex-wife with a terminal illness, who wants to repair relations and say goodbye, but he's not sure which ex-wife it is, Ginny or Jenny. A friend tells him about meeting the wife of a man executed by the state. But these scenes don't reek of death, even if I might be giving that impression. Instead, they circle death with care and earned levity.

The final story, "Doppelgänger, Poltergeist," features several enfolded plots that ripple outward in beguiling and concentric patterns. One is about a writer and his former student, Marcus Ahearn. Another is about a husband and wife who enjoy erotic visitations from the ghost of Elvis Presley. The former student, Ahearn, is obsessed with Elvis and his stillborn twin, who, perhaps by some shady miracle, didn't die at birth but was stolen by a midwife, lived, and was later swapped in by Elvis's manager, "Colonel" Tom Parker, when Elvis was drafted into the military in 1958. This theory would account for the dramatic transformation of Elvis from young sex god to flabby and self-destructive cipher. The idea is that maybe the two phases we know of Elvis's were so extremely different because they were lived by different people: brothers who shared the womb. We learn that Ahearn's older brother, a collector of Elvis records, had been, like Elvis, the sole survivor of a pair of twins—a fact that allows Ahearn, in a bout of fevered logic, to suggest that his teacher, the story's narrator, is his own older brother's lost, possibly undead identical sibling. Denis Johnson riffs gamefully with all this, but he is playing for keeps. It seems reasonable to guess that he knew he was at the end of his life when he wrote this story. Knew he would soon be "leaving the building" himself, but would ponder, first, the possibility that another king, of another genre, had managed to disappear behind an everlasting mystery. It's natural to hope for an encore, until you're told from on high that the artist is really and truly gone. And even then.

IN THE COMPANY
OF TRUCKERS

One summer in the late 1990s I was driving across the country on I-80, having just stopped to visit some friends in Des Moines, Iowa. I was behind the wheel of a 1963 Chevrolet Impala I'd bought outside Asheville, North Carolina. The car ran well and was beautiful—champagne body with a cream top, no dents, no rust, and no one had done anything stupid to it. I remember vividly that the interior had these plastic disks, like thin translucent washers, that fit between the window roller and door panel, to keep the upholstery from being indented or pinched; that's how pristine, how undefiled, that car was. I was planning to sell it in Los Angeles, where a '63 Impala in such cherry condition would fetch several times what I paid for it.

It had been later than I'd hoped, maybe four p.m., when I'd said goodbye to my friends in Des Moines and got on I-80. Everything felt fine despite the heavy sky, which seemed to go almost black on the horizon as I headed west. I remembered what an Iowan, a guy named Johnny Coin who lived a bit like he was in the movie *Apocalypse Now*, had said to me once about the weather in that state: "It's like Vietnam." I was crossing into Nebraska as I hit a wall of rain. I slowed to thirty miles an hour with a thick sheet of water pouring over the car. I've had old cars that leak around the windshield; this one did not. It had working heat and AC, a functioning radio, intact weather stripping, wipers—these things are luxury and civilization in an antique car. It's chamber music: you feel on top of the world when you're dry and moving along in a downpour. In a new car, in which everything is plastic and somewhat ugly and works today but will break eventually, there's no thrill to function.

But then there was no function: the car cut out. Cleanly. No sputter, no de-acceleration, just *click*. It was off, and slowing. I moved right, but heavily, because the car's power steering was out. By a stroke of luck, there was an exit just up ahead. I willed the car enough momentum to roll to the exit. It did. It rolled right into a truck stop.

I know only the most rudimentary things, mechanically speaking. I can lift the hood and check and add oil, aim carb cleaner in the general direction where it's supposed to go, but really that's it. I lifted the hood and stood there. The rain had let up, but it was getting dark. This was before cell phones, and, in my life, at least, it was before the invention of the credit card and AAA roadside service. Several truckers came over and stood around the open hood. Various theories were suggested, but no one seemed to really know what the trouble was. A petite and wiry man walked up, grim faced, carrying one of those Igloo coolers that is for six beers, with the top ripped off. It was filled with a jumble of greasy tools. The others nodded in his direction and someone said, "There's your guy."

They backed away, one by one, as the wiry little man began a methodical inspection of my car. I'll confess I was disappointed by his junky-looking tools, but the others had acted like a messiah had arrived. The man did not acknowledge me. He simply went to work, as the rain began to fall again. Soon, we were both soaking wet.

He was disconnecting my exhaust manifold when a tow truck driver got involved. The starter was bad, and because the Impala had custom headers, they had to be removed to get to it. The tow truck driver, a big chubby man who told me to call him "Snacker," said he had the keys to a parts warehouse sixty miles east and would go and get the replacement starter I needed and charge me only cost.

The wiry trucker and I went inside and drank sour coffee as we waited for Snacker to return. The trucker insisted on paying for my coffee. He never made eye contact. I said, "You're so kind to help me, and you won't even let me buy your coffee." He said, almost impatiently, "I have a daughter."

But the thing is, he wasn't old enough to be my father. Now I'm married to the son of a trucker, from an entire family of truckers, although my father-in-law died, at the young age of forty-six, before I got to meet him. One of his brothers, whom I did know, spent his final hours of life shifting gears on a hospital gurney, unaware he wasn't operating his eighteen-wheeler.

When Snacker returned it was late, maybe ten p.m. The trucker proceeded to install the new starter and reconnect the exhaust, a task that—with the car not on a lift but on the ground, in the rain, in the middle of the night—was not enviable. When the trucker was finished bolting the exhaust manifold, he had grease in his eyes. My car still would not start. After a lengthy diagnosis, me standing there, soaked to the skin, he said there was a bad part in the electronic ignition (not an original feature, and thus someone *had* done something stupid to that car), which had fried the original starter and needed to be replaced.

Snacker, now part of our one-night team, angelically agreed to go east once more, a 120-mile round trip, to get the module I needed. The trucker said, "I'll get everything ready for when he returns. You go sleep in my rig." I protested. It seemed selfish to sleep when he, a perfect stranger, was working on my car. He insisted. "You have to drive to California tomorrow and that's a long way. Get some sleep." It seemed like it would bother him less if I complied, so I did, instead of pointing out that he had a tanker of chemicals that surely needed to be delivered someplace.

If you haven't slept in a trucker's cab, I can tell you the interior is fancier than you might imagine. His special trucker alarm (almost impossible to turn off) blared at five a.m. The trucker himself was on the floor, below the slim bed. He was shirtless, with what I seem to recall was a hand towel draped over him like a sad little blanket. As we both got up, we said nothing, made no eye contact, just like the night before.

The rain had stopped, and the sun was coming up when Snacker returned with the magical little part. The trucker installed it and reconnected everything. The car rumbled to life when I turned the key. Snacker whooped.

The trucker said, "Go, you're set—that's it." I stayed there. I could not leave. I said, "I must pay you. You worked all night on my car." But I had given all I had besides gas money to Snacker for the parts. "No," he said, "no way." I begged him to give me his address. I was crying. It could have been lack of sleep, but it was also a moment when I understood what it means to be overwhelmed by kindness. He refused and mentioned his daughter again, and it felt like my insistence would disrupt an entire system by which he was operating. You do things sometimes for a stranger. You simply do them.

I left. I remember the angle of the early morning sun as I pulled out of that truck stop. More things happened that day and the next, more kindness from people I did not know, and some lack of kindness, and then, in the afternoon a day later, I crossed into California. I was on the part of I-80 where it starts to lope along next to the Truckee River.

A group of boys was on the side of the road, shirtless, with towels draped around their necks. One of them put out his thumb as I passed. He did it playfully, I suspected, but I stopped anyway, backed up the shoulder, and offered them a ride. I don't know exactly how many there were but a lot. Six or seven. They piled in, and the car sank on its springs. One gave directions of where to drop them, but when we got there, a house with a bunch of kids skateboarding in front, my passengers said actually it wasn't where they needed to go, and waved tauntingly at their friends as we gunned it. They did this twice more. I didn't mind. They wanted to be seen in a dope ride. We drove around Truckee as they hung their arms out the windows and signaled to people they knew. I complied willingly but understood this was not my big chance to help a stranger, or strangers. This was too much fun.

BAD CAPTAINS

My aspiration to spend time at sea as requisite literary training died long ago, on a white-knuckled ferry ride to Elba during a torrential rainstorm. Not only was I seasick; I saw the population on board as hostile competitors to salvation. As the ferry lurched and rolled, we gave one another dirty looks, sized up whose head we would push under the waves to keep our own above the waterline. The thin membrane of civility frayed with every jerk and jolt, and "the law of the sea," from the literature I loved most, seemed nowhere to be found.

And so, this past summer, when I boarded a fast boat to Capri—that famous rock where Lenin and Adorno hiked, and where now those who can afford prices set for Russian oligarchs shop—I was not immune to the prospect that the good-looking captain in his tight white slacks might throw us to the sharks. I had decided that it is the fate of my generation never to have known the noble law of the sea, and to live, instead, in an era when the captain leaves his ship not last but first. Call it the new spirit of capitalism, ushered in with all the other forms of ruthlessness that mark contemporary times, and painted into our naval history most vividly, and recently, by the tragedy of the *Costa Concordia* and its notorious captain, Francesco Schettino.

Schettino is tanned, with glittering ice-blue eyes and black lustrous hair, hair in which, apparently, traces of cocaine were found. He has a full-blooded and virile affect, and he exudes intense vanity. This vanity pours in where intelligence might be absent or might have vacated itself, at least temporarily, to accommodate such vanity, which argues for its own permanent residence in the mind and in the genitals, where there is plenty of room.

A few hours after the seventeen-deck *Costa Concordia* set sail, everything routine, Captain Schettino gave an order for the ship to slow down so that he could enjoy to the full his dessert and drain the decanter of red wine he was sharing with his twenty-five-year-old blond Moldovan stowaway. He then reported to the bridge for his off-course and showy flyby of the island of Giglio.

That evening—Friday the thirteenth, January 2012—Captain Schettino jumped or "fell" into a lifeboat. This happened early in a long night of harrowing rescues. Schettino was conspicuously dry and on land while many hundreds of his passengers were still on board; or sliding down ropes past the ship's enormous port-side flank; or jumping thirty feet into the water and attempting to swim for land; or helpless and praying, being either old or infirm or with children too young to climb down ropes; or, after slipping on fuel-sloshed and tilting decks, found themselves trapped in the depths of the ship, where the water was rising. Thirty-two passengers died that night, by drowning or from hypothermia.

The island of Giglio, Schettino's planned if unofficial flyby, was where the *Costa Concordia* hit a rock, Schettino having failed, or refused, to take proper soundings. Which is pretty much what happened on the morning of July 2, 1816, when an inexperienced minor aristocrat who'd been made captain of the French frigate *Medusa* piloted the ship into shallow water near the coast of Senegal.

As crew members noted, the waters into which the *Medusa* was sailing were ominously warm. The captain did not take note. The sea went green, and crew members worried. The captain did not. Sand scrolled in the waves. Floating cities of kelp appeared: trouble, crew members knew. The sea went clear: they were screwed. The *Medusa* ran aground on the treacherous Arguin Bank. Chaos ensued. The captain abandoned ship and, worse, cut the rope to the makeshift raft of 147 survivors he had pledged to tow from a rescue boat. On the abandoned raft, murder, insanity, and cannibalism ensued. There was a lot of begging to be thrown into the boiling sea. There was mutiny, and crazed guzzling of wine, and rash and desperate sawing at the raft's lashings. The only provisions and most of the people were tossed. When, after thirteen days, the survivors were finally rescued, only 17 of 147 were left.

Like the captain of the *Medusa*, Schettino became a national disgrace for having sneaked off his ship. He caused unnecessary deaths and ruined a $570 million cruise liner (which would cost more than a billion dollars to scrap). And he destroyed—very nearly—a section of coastline and the livelihood of the Italians who live on the island where the *Concordia* capsized. Also, he was a coward, a serious offense in Italy.

"*Vada a bordo, cazzo!*" a Livorno coast guard captain had yelled at Schettino, the call famously recorded, then played and replayed: *Vada a bordo, Vada a bordo.* I wouldn't want to get back on board. Who would? It doesn't seem so pleasant, to have to go down with the ship. It's not at all tempting. But going down with the ship is the ethical prescription of the profession Schettino chose. Never mind modern law and coastal jurisdictions: this is about ancient writ. Schettino refused the sublime injunction to sacrifice himself. Unlike Conrad's Jim, whose moral lapse, abandoning the *Patna*, is later redeemed, Schettino, at this point, has found himself no empathetic Marlow. He is not "one of us." We are obliged to have contempt for him, and we do.

In *Journey to the End of the Night*, Céline's narrator, Ferdinand Bardamu, describes the captain of the boat he is on: "a shady, breezy, racketeering type," who "had gone out of his way to shake hands with me at the start." Bardamu boards the *Admiral Bragueton* in Marseille, heading for Africa. In the heat and fetid air of the tropics, the other passengers congeal into drunkenness. With their flabby movements they look like squid. Meanwhile Bardamu develops delusions of grandeur, imagining that in the alcoholism, moral collapse, sexual frustration, and cosmic boredom on the ship, a seething and plotting among his fellow passengers has taken place, in which Bardamu has been identified as a kind of Schettino among them: an enemy and scapegoat who the other passengers have tacitly decided must be cornered and destroyed, or at least thrown overboard.

The year before the *Costa Concordia* fell on its side and killed thirty-two people, it starred in a movie. Jean-Luc Godard's *Film socialisme* has gambling and a brunch buffet, frantic disco, the banter of history, vanished gold, Palestine. Shot in HD, the footage transforms the enormous cruise liner into something mythical—dazzling, clean, massive, magnificent. There is the brilliant blue and rich yellow of its broad, glossy decks and gigantic smokestack. The sparkling white of its bulk and the froth of its glorious wake. The ship is the dream, the passengers its dreamers.

In one scene, the French philosopher Alain Badiou gives a talk on Husserl and geometry to an empty lecture hall on the ship, as if Badiou, too, is dreaming: the philosopher who doesn't notice that there is no audience (or who understands that he is awake while others sleep, and can do nothing to rouse them). Godard's film is divided into three parts. The first and third take place on the *Concordia*, but the third also interjects, into the ports at which the *Concordia* stops, historic newsreel and film images. When the ship arrives in Naples, Godard quotes, unattributed, Curzio Malaparte's novel *The Skin*: "The 'plague' had broken out in Naples on October 1, 1943." The plague is the Americans, who arrived that day along with their American so-called freedom, the presence or promise of which turns every woman, Malaparte chides, into a prostitute and every man into a scheming wretch. *The Skin* celebrates, perversely and relentlessly, the desperation of Neapolitans, their double-edged gratitude to their American "liberators." Naples, Malaparte declares, "the only city in the world that did not founder in the colossal shipwreck of ancient civilization," has survived only to face genuine ruin when the Americans arrive with their health, cheer, clean morals, tight-fitting uniforms, and their outrageous contradictions. But as Godard shows us, in his majestic views of the *Concordia* as an unearthly, glistening iceberg, pure and whole, the plague can be beautiful.

The cruise ship, Jonathan Franzen told the *Paris Review* in 2010, is "emblematic of our time." I doubted this, despite the witty reportage of David Foster Wallace's essay on their nearly lethal comforts and the high artistry of Franzen's extended cruise scene in *The Corrections*. I considered luxury liners an example of middlebrow surrealism, certainly not emblematic. But they keep coming into view. They monster-glide up the Giudecca Canal, intruding into the old, watery dream-state that is Venice, continuing to dwarf the campanile of St. Mark's Basilica even after the catastrophe of the *Concordia*.

In truth the cruise ship is lodged deeper in my thoughts than I want to admit. As a child, I was a devoted reader of *Mad* magazine. My first issue (161, September 1973) featured a spoof called "The Poopsidedown Adventure," about a luxury liner that sinks. I read that issue so many times—a manual and master text, as I thought of it, for understanding adult humor—that I had it almost memorized:

> "Listen to me everybody! We've turned over! If we want to be saved, we've got to go up to the bottom!!"
> "Up to the bottom?!"
> "Yes . . . UP to the BOTTOM! Because all the people who are down on top are DEAD!!"
> "We've got to work our way up to the propeller room!"
> "Yeah? And what will we get there?"
> "The shaft!!"
> "Now, we'll need something to climb up! I know! We'll use that fallen Christmas tree! It's going to be hard climbing it, with its sharp metal ornaments, shorted lights and rickety frame! But it's a sacrifice God wants us to make!"

For years I considered the *Mad* version the real story and assumed the Hollywood movie *The Poseidon Adventure* was just some spinoff. I didn't know the movie, had no way to see it, and wanted my experience to be, as it felt to me, *direct*. The real *Poseidon Adventure* is apparently an allegory of capitalism's collapse, though I still haven't seen it.

The *Costa Concordia* is not an allegory. But as in *The Poseidon Adventure*, there was corruption in the structure up above. The ship, which is owned by the American supercompany Carnival, apparently had a cheap, thin hull, which slashed open too easily.

"I am not ashamed to say that I pushed people and used my fists to secure a place," one passenger later said. "I started yelling at people," said a volunteer from the town who went on board to save lives. He was described as ruggedly handsome (nine-tenths of those who come to the aid of survivors in such emergencies, locals who feel the urgent call to heroism as a natural instinct, are later described as ruggedly handsome). "'Don't be animals! Stop being animals!' I shouted this many times, to allow the children in. It had no effect." Two years later, the ferry MV *Sewol* capsized off the south coast of Korea while the captain was in his quarters, smoking in his underwear. He was one of the first to be rescued. Three hundred and four passengers, most of them high school students, drowned.

The 1980s television show *The Love Boat* offered new passengers and new problems to unknot each week. It is a verso to Godard's *Film socialisme*, which is the same banal cruise-line reverie, except seen, through Godard's lens, with weird grace. But Godard also filmed via spy cameras, surveillance cameras, and phones. The effect of these views is a depersonalized *Love Boat*: a boat without the love stories and with a set of real passengers who are accidental extras. "Poor Europe," one of Godard's characters says, "not purified, but corrupted by suffering. Not exalted, but humiliated by recaptured liberty." There's no possibility here of a one-hour resolution.

Meanwhile, the *Love Boat* "soon will be making another run," as the theme song goes. No one on board is worried about historic suffering. And not only that, but love *won't hurt anymore*.

Plague-free, this love on offer. A love that won't hurt anymore. What a promise.

Was that song in my head as the fast boat I'd boarded in Naples passed the island of Ischia, where love and cruelty batter Lenù in Elena

Ferrante's novels, and neared Meta di Sorrento, Captain Schettino's hometown, before sloshing to a stop at the port in Capri? No. The only thing in my head was coping in the human swarm, the pushing and the shoving toward luxury-brand luggage and then the exit.

Luckily, a natural order, a consensual and even elegant hierarchy, took hold: there were professional basketball players on our boat, and they got off first.

HAPPY HOUR

I f you take the persona of the artist Jeff Koons at face value and figure him to be effusive and seductive but also innocent, a bit like William Gaddis's fictive eleven-year-old money genius, J R Vansant, you might expect the voice of this man Jeff Koons to be smooth, upbeat, and boyish. Buoyant and motivational. A voice as slick as his mirror-polished balloon dog, the single artwork everybody knows— even children know the balloon dog, even grown-ups who disdain contemporary art. Jeff Koons, after all, is a man of the people—this despite being a visual artist, a career generally met with suspicion, if not derision. But Koons is different. He's a showman and salesman, keeping the dream of American entrepreneurial success alive.

And yet, as I discovered the first time I heard the actual, real voice of Jeff Koons, as he explained various of his artworks ("these twins from hard-core porn look just like Elvis"; "the mustache on this lobster refers to Duchamp"), it was a voice, to my surprise, that was hoarse and low. It had so much doubt and rasp to it that I could not match it to the beaming, gleaming, schoolboy face of the world's most famous artist.

In 1975, Jeff Koons interviewed the musician David Byrne. There is a video of their conversation on YouTube, which for some reason shows only Koons. Byrne, the subject, is off-screen. Koons has a mustache and sideburns. His face is coated in a sheen of nervous sweat, or maybe it's just summertime-in–New York sweat. Regardless, this brief bit of vintage footage is a rare glimpse of Koons without the camera-ready perfection we've come to know, the manicured Ken doll in a soft collared shirt or a dark and expensive suit or a tuxedo, beaming with his eyes open a little too wide.

In this 1975 video, his eyes frequently narrow in amusement as he chews gum, endures awkward silences, cracks a sly grin. He tells David Byrne he's from central Pennsylvania, his words spoken with some kind of central Pennsylvania accent. "They have Bird-in-Hand, Cherryville, Pleasureville," he says. These are the names of towns, enunciated for irony. Maybe he and Byrne are both stoned on weak 1970s weed. We hear a toilet flush.

David Byrne: "Things go on in other towns, but it's more secret. Here, you can pay to see those things."

Koons, with disdain: "Where I'm from, that's all they have is middle-class bars." Later he tells Byrne about a bar he went to that he liked, in Baltimore, on New Year's Eve, a strip club with nude girls. It was "comfortable," he says, and "real." At which point Byrne changes the subject.

The seamless and clean-cut salesman persona that Jeff Koons has confected over the last thirty years is a long way from this greaser with a mustache longing for what's "comfortable" and "real" about a Baltimore titty joint. The young Koons seemed like he wanted to be cool, and he was cool: he was interviewing one of the hippest downtown musicians. He wasn't yet performing his man-child consumerism, claiming that happiness, to him, "is a full box of cereal and a full carton of milk." But some of Koons's own artwork has interfered with his breakfast cereal persona too.

I'm thinking in particular of the series *Luxury and Degradation*, which features exact reproductions, in oil on canvas, of liquor advertisements that were contemporary when Koons made them, in 1986. The paintings pair well-known slogans—"I could go for something Gordon's" and "I assume you drink Martell"—with staged images, combinations whose effects are both curiously meaningless and strangely charged. Replicated and monumentalized as art, they are not bubblegum Koons— dazzle that masquerades as innocence and puerility, under which lies a kind of darkness, even nastiness—and instead, flat and caustic at once.

Hard liquor is not the aesthetic or spiritual hearth of a feel-good world, the mirror in which people want to see themselves. Even if liquor does hold some promise of revelry, of escape, the ads for it are a mediated layer away from that. They are corporate fictions that do not ignite privately stored memories from good times, bad times, or any times. Mostly, they ignite memories of *looking at the ads themselves*— in magazines, on roadway billboards, or elsewhere—giving a sense of déjà vu. (What is being done to me? Something, but I can't name it.)

Koons himself, whenever discussing *Luxury and Degradation*— in a MoMA lecture, in a TV documentary made about him—seems habitually to absent the conjunction, saying instead, "*Luxury Degradation*," suggesting that one modifies the other, the degradation of luxury, or luxurious degradation. A lot of Koons's works, giant puppies made of flowers, or Michael Jackson cuddling his pet chimp Bubbles, or the bows, hearts, and balloon dogs of his series *Celebration*, are about gazing upon images and objects that reflect back as splendid and universal—or so the account goes of Koons's populist appeal. Everybody loves puppies and hearts and ribbons. They're universal. Liquor, too, is universal. But it isn't a touchstone of carefree moments. And thus the pieces in *Luxury and Degradation* don't contribute to Koons's undisputed status as the artist most loved by children, a Bernini for the masses with a monopoly on the kitsch-sublime. Children who can say unabashedly that the giant puppy in flowers is art would not know that the liquor ads are art. And because the liquor ads are such uninflected appropriation—reprints in oil on canvas of the originals—the average museumgoer may see the ads as generational, nostalgic, but remain unsure what they are, what they are doing. And without that nostalgic layer—let's pretend it's 1986, and these ads are contemporary—what is the effect?

This body of work also includes fabricated stainless-steel replicas of liquor company "collectibles," such as Jim Beam miniatures of a steam train and a Model A Ford, as well as a travel bar based on one that Koons's father, a furniture salesman and interior decorator, apparently owned. What person ever used a travel bar? No one. Characters in Eudora Welty and Flannery O'Connor stories use travel bars. Lonely salesmen who die unattended on the side of the road.

Koons's steam train is a set of cars cast in stainless steel, the material used in fermentation vats, filled with whiskey, and sealed with a tax stamp. Break the seal, enjoy the liquor, and you get a perfect lesson in art's auratic qualities: you drink the value, wreck the art. Koons's own comment about the materials he chose was that stainless steel looks fancy but is proletarian, "what pots and pans are made of." But the kitsch objects he's copying are proletarian to begin with, now downsized (and transubstantiated) into a limited number of artworks that will not be flooding eBay and the shelves of thrift stores, as the original "collectibles" do.

If we made a star map of appropriation, advertising, alcohol, and America, we could plot the obvious points: Jasper Johns (who replicated cans of Ballantine Ale in solid bronze); Andy Warhol (who joked that he could have been even more famous if only cult leader Jim Jones had poisoned his followers with Campbell's soup instead of Flavor Aid); Richard Prince (whose Marlboro Man evokes addiction and premature death as rugged individualism, iconography, men and the West); Cady Noland (who, like Richard Prince, evokes iconography, men and the West—but as chain-link fencing, Budweiser cans, barricades, ripped flags). Meanwhile, Koons's liquor ads are not a commentary, nor are they an ironic appropriation. They are a straight appropriation. While Prince is emphasizing the power of the myth and Noland is draining myth to the bottom of the vat, Koons is replicating the myth itself, in its seemingly empty formality.

The liquor ads are mysterious and ambivalent. They are plain old advertising and, like advertising, flat and ungiving. They take a moment that is pretend-eternal in its representation of an idea, a demographic or fantasy demographic, and they redouble that moment: render it brighter and more garish—but, as ever, eternally mute. Since Vance Packard's 1957 book *The Hidden Persuaders*, we've all understood that ads use varying degrees of nuance to seed desire. Packard opened the discourse on the power of suggestion. Later came *Subliminal Seduction* (1974) by Wilson Bryan Key, who saw satanic imagery in the ice cubes of liquor ads and the word "sex" imprinted on the surface of Ritz crackers—providing, unwittingly, a perfect straw man for the ad industry, which could claim Key was a lunatic. Urban legend of the seventies had it that grocery stores played hidden messages in their Muzak, asking customers, sotto voce, not to steal.

One could argue that the Cold War made everyone paranoid about mind control, but the cunning of the marketplace, the structural requirement for demand, gives all the cause a person needs to feel manipulated. Advertisers are sophisticated, at least about the people they hire: those with quick minds and a deft understanding of the relation between language and image. It's no accident that William

Gaddis wrote text for corporate brochures and that Don DeLillo produced copy for Ogilvy & Mather.

The liquor ads that Koons chose to reproduce, a process that involved going to the original agencies and borrowing the printing plates for each image, are all staged scenes with semidetached captions. The words float free but remain inside the frame of the image. Each advertisement is a scene, a make-believe-realist portrait of contrived life, which functions as a sort of temporal hinge, pointing to what might have just been taking place and, more important, what will happen next. The caption, meanwhile, guides us to an interpretation of what we see and what we can intuit as imminent. It is choreography. And we are choreography too: trained to read these things in a certain way. Commercials utilize configurations of men and women in tableaux of "hyper-ritualization," as the sociologist Erving Goffman calls it. Ingrained in us is the index to the signals we see. Also ingrained in us is the instinct to decode the scene. But the decoding requires small leaps. The scenes lack information. They are oblique, truncated, and in some cases abstract.

"I assume you drink Martell," the attractive virago with shining white eyes says. I remember this ad. It was on billboards all over America in the mid-1980s. *You assumed correctly, lady friend.* Whatever she assumes is fine. It doesn't matter what she assumes. The answer is yes.

"I could go for something Gordon's." The man tugs on the woman's shirttail as she dips her brush, an easel before her. They're on the beach. She's trying to paint. He's trying to distract her. *I love it when you play like you have a hobby. You're beautiful when you're concentrating. You're cute when you're serious. When you insist on this . . . plein air thing. Also I love your "tabula rasa" low-cut white-on-white outfit, which is waiting to get splattered with . . . ocean spray? A bit of paint?* He plays the gentle, supportive companion who will bide his time until he can transition from the (playacted) role of sidekick, doing nothing but enjoying the negative ions at the beach while she paints, to his real position as dominant enabler, who pours her a drink. Screw the paints and the easel, I could go for something Gordon's (how many steps away is the beach house, unseen in this image, but the point of retreat that the something he could go for involves?).

The company had another ad in the same series, a similar couple, good-looking young professionals, reading different parts of a newspaper that is spread over the floor in some kind of magnificent domicile, huge and unfurnished. Trying to decode what kind of space it is, I'm reminded of a comment in *Amazons*, a novel DeLillo wrote under a pseudonym, that "apartments sprawl," while "houses ramble." We are in the territory of the sell. The couple lounges around in a sprawling apartment somewhere on the East Coast (he's wearing sockless loafers). It's clearly Sunday, given the size of the newspaper dismantled on the floor. He touches her hair with the end of his pencil. It's the same gesture, if a different pair of actors/models, as the light tug on the shirttail at the beach. It's, *Stop pretending to finish that* Times *crossword puzzle*. What happens next is off-screen, but on the screens of our imagining. Not anything explicit. Just possibility.

What else does Gordon's make besides alcohol? Nothing. So the message is: let's drink. But also: female ambition must be neutralized for happy relations. Then again, it could be she who is saying it. "I could go for *X*." Meaning, I wasn't serious about this. Let's pretend for five or ten more minutes that I was serious and then let's go for something Gordon's.

A similar message comes through in the Hennessy ad Koons chose to replicate. The man has been up late working on the briefs for an especially tough case. He's the lawyer, the arbiter, the judge. She's the partner, wife, paralegal, or girlfriend. But she's tired of waiting around while he insists on acting out his ego needs, to be ambitious and preoccupied. Come on, honey, join me for a nightcap. That's where the message comes in: his work is not done. He can still litigate, legislate, judge. Justice can be served, but with his woman, while putting his case to rest. "The civilized way to lay down the law."

From two terms of Obama's counterterrorism policy, we learned that the "civilized" way to lay down the law was with drone strikes, not Hennessy. But let's try to look at what this could mean, in the ad, as a floating message synchronous with its image. The realm is that of domestic law, not juridical or geopolitical—patriarchal, but imposed not on children, only women.

Koons himself has called these works "sociological" evidence of the different income levels the companies target, brand to brand and ad to ad. The ad campaigns, Koons has commented, veer toward "abstraction" at the higher levels, the upper social classes.

"I just rode the subways here in New York. And I would go from one economic area, from Harlem, to the other, Grand Central Station. I got the whole spectrum of advertising. You deal with the lowest economic base to the highest level. I realized how the level of visual abstraction is changing. The more money comes into play, the more abstract."

Koons's example of this upper-level "abstraction" is a Frangelico ad, a liquid amber background and the words "Stay in Tonight." No people. No dramatic tableau. It's almost a monochrome.

"It was like they were using abstraction to debase you, because they always want to debase you."

Koons's linking of refinement with debasement recalls Joan Didion's closing comment in her essay on the Getty Villa, which, she says, serves as "a palpable contract between the very rich and the people who distrust them the least." Tacky and overt signs of luxury are for the poor. Tasteful, subdued signs of luxury are for the rich. But the very richest do not buy Frangelico. They buy Jeff Koons paintings of liquor advertisements, sure that they are in on the joke, which is how any palpable contract—between peddler and consumer, artist and critic, artist and collector—functions best.

In a mise en abyme of these dyads, the Whitney Museum catalog for the Jeff Koons retrospective included an in situ image of *I Could Go for Something Gordon's* in the living room of a collector's lavish mansion in Greenwich, Connecticut. The Gordon's ad is huge, above a colonial revival marble fireplace. Its acid hues—the red and yellow Gordon's distillery label, a slice of lime—are next to a wall dominated by an abstract Gerhard Richter painting in the same registers of fire red, sun yellow, and lime green. Koons and Richter, low and a version of high, neutralize each other on adjacent walls.

But these aren't just any walls, even among the small and rarefied world of the obnoxious rich. This is the home of disgraced former Whitney Museum trustee Warren B. Kanders, who has made a fortune from "defense equipment"—body armor, and "less lethal" weapons including stinger grenades and tear gas. Tear gas canisters traced back to his parent company, Safariland, were fired on migrants, including women and children, on the US border with Mexico in the fall of 2018.

At the height of a roiling controversy, before Kanders ultimately resigned from the Whitney board—and well before Safariland tear gas canisters were fired on crowds of American protestors in cities small and large across this country after the murder of George Floyd—I found myself in a social situation that included a different Whitney trustee, at a dinner party where this trustee felt comfortable and assumed she was with her own kind. (One of the many ironies of the art world is the palpable contract between the wealthy who sustain the art and artists who make it. The lowly writer, outside this contract, is nonetheless occasionally summoned to appear, paid in dinner, and expected to behave.) This trustee, a woman in a silver bubble jacket, assured me that "Tear gas is not only *necessary* but sometimes it's really quite desirable!" The civilized way to lay down the law. "I mean, imagine if we didn't have it!" She invoked Ferguson and other "scary" situations. I transitioned away from her and poured myself a drink.

What the trustee meant to make explicit, without having to spell it out—because why should this woman in a silver bubble jacket, esteemed patron of the arts, have to speak in a language not graced with nuance, given that abstraction, after all, is the language of the rich?—what she really meant to communicate to me was that the alternative to tear gas was shooting people, and with live ammunition, and at least none of the trustees were involved in that!

TRAMPING IN THE BYWAYS

My connection to a strange little book called *How I Became One of the Invisible* by David Rattray is through the people who occupy its first hundred pages. These are people who occupied the first hundred pages of my own life, some as ghosts, others as flesh and blood, and loomed large to me as they did to David Rattray. They are, principally: Johnny Sherrill, who Rattray introduces as a bit like Mezz Mezzrow (translation: a white man with a black man's soul) and a bit like a character who stepped from the pages of Jean Genet's *The Thief's Journal* (translation: a cool cat who'd been in prison); and Alden Van Buskirk, who was gifted with angelic looks and natural poetic talent, and cursed with a rare and fatal blood disease that killed him at twenty-three. Rattray had been the only person to commit Johnny and Alden—or Van, as he was sometimes called—and the particular worlds both occupied, to print. He was not the person to whom either of them was closest, but he understood that they were special and rare individuals who deserved their slots in posterity.

My own link to this book is almost coincidental, deriving from the pure luck of being born to my parents (and aren't we all tired of those born lucky? Well, at least I wasn't born rich). Rattray himself would not have been keen on the idea of coincidence, a concept he would find too sober and positivist. He would, instead, read *meaning* into coincidence. And the truth is, I do too.

Rattray—as I always heard him called, and never David nor Dave—was a friend of my father's from Dartmouth College. He was older than my father by a handful of years and they overlapped only briefly, in 1956, when my father and Alden, both freshmen, both on the ski team, met Rattray just before he fled to Paris, chasing European bohemia. My father and Alden had immediately bonded when they arrived at college, sharing a love of poetry and jazz and skiing. Dartmouth, in those years, had a poetry series run by Richard Eberhart, who invited Jack Hirschman, Kenneth Rexroth, Robert Creeley, W. D. Snodgrass, and I. A. Richards to read to a small group, which included my father and Alden.

The year they were freshmen, Eberhart went out to San Francisco, heard Ginsberg read an early version of "Howl," and wrote about it in the *New York Times*. (Eberhart also apparently advised Ginsberg to add something positive, to counterbalance the poem's litanies, which Ginsberg did, in the form of its famous footnote of "holy holy holys"). Rattray, meanwhile, went to St. Elizabeths Hospital in Washington, DC, to interview Ezra Pound, who was, at the time, impounded there. Rattray was twenty-one years old, but even at that young age, he possessed the skill and strategic wisdom to let Pound reveal himself, casually and naturally, without interference. Pound enveloped Rattray in a caul of solicitude, offering a long list of contacts on Provençal literature, rantings on the peril of hocking one's mansion to a Jew, and insane asylum cafeteria food, which, as Rattray figured out, Pound was providing as daily nourishment to his coterie of groupies, one of whom, "Queen of the Beats" Sheri Martinelli, was busy sketching Pound as he expounded to Rattray. The exchange was written up as an uproariously funny and disturbing view into the mind and utterances of the grand old modernist, with his giant calves, which looked to Rattray like legs you'd see on an old sailor, "still spry from climbing the rigging," his by turns gallant and jagged manner, and his consistent champagne flow of bigoted spew.

Rattray was from a quasi-aristocratic East Coast lineage, an inheritance of perhaps a good deal of baggage and not a whole lot of dough. He "spoke prose," as my father put it: non-idiomatic formal English. His grandfather had been a whaler by profession off the coast of Long Island. His sister was an early bohemian who spent her time traveling the world by ocean liner and ran a vintage boutique on St. Mark's Place. She lived in a mansion in East Hampton. While staying there my father once encountered the poet Delmore Schwartz, also a houseguest. At the time, my father was a graduate student in philosophy, which Delmore Schwartz had himself studied. They talked for three hours about J. L. Austin. On that visit or another, Rattray took my father to see his grandfather's whaling boat, which was stored in an old commercial warehouse in Sag Harbor. It looked like a large canoe, long and slim, with oars—no engine. A whale would have been harpooned from this primitive vessel, and then dragged behind it for miles, until, exhausted, it would finally expire.

The first thing I ever read of Rattray's was not the legendary "A Weekend with Ezra Pound," but an essay called "Van," which begins with Rattray's introduction to Alden Van Buskirk. Rattray was immediately transfixed. Alden had that effect on people in his short life, and also after it. As Rattray narrates, he and Alden set out together for Mexico, "a journey to the edge of the world" in the Burroughs and Kerouac mode of drugs and discovery.

They go to a place called Puerto Angel, which they chose for the name.

As they lie in hammocks, Rattray imagines them in a late-nineteenth-century engraving, with the title *Tramping in the Byways of Oaxaca*. When I first read Rattray's account of Puerto Angel, of him and Alden quickly escaping after they'd ripped off the drug-addicted local constable, I was given an alternate view on someone I'd been hearing about my whole life. My brother's middle name is Alden, in memoriam. (In "Harvest," Rattray says Johnny Sherrill will name his son Alden, in tribute, but this seems to be Rattray's mix-up with my brother. Johnny's son is Gary William Sherrill, a lifelong family friend.) My mother and my father were each separately friends with Alden, and they met each other, and connected, and then had children, via their Alden-commonality, and so I more or less consider him the patron saint of my parents' common-law "marriage," as well as my and my brother's existences.

We had no religion or traditions in our house. We had an assortment of characters who took up residence in our lives, and we had books, among them Alden's posthumous collection of poetry, *Lami*, which Rattray had the dedicated ingenuity to collate and send to Allen Ginsberg, who was impressed enough to write an introduction and secure a publisher. Alden's "widow," Martha Muhs, was a friend and regular visitor. Johnny Sherrill was as well. Alden, despite having died so long ago, has remained a regular reference and spirit among my parents and their friends, who witnessed his beauty, energy, insights.

In 1960, Alden had moved to St. Louis, where he had first encountered Johnny Sherrill. In "Van," Johnny is described by Rattray as a thirty-year-old ex-convict who makes his living "scamming, jamming, pimping, gambling, doing time," and who "identified with everything that had soul." All true, except maybe the pimping. "He *wishes* he was a pimp," my mother says when I ask her about Rattray's immortalizing of Johnny. If Johnny strutted like a pimp, it was more a citation of a pimp than a *pimp*-pimp. He was a trickster, not a salesman.

Johnny was a skilled machinist by trade, if also an itinerant carouser, joker, drinker, wordsmith, and lady's man. Johnny had robbed a train at the age of seventeen and gone to prison, where he learned machining. Rattray describes him as the son of migrant fruit pickers and says his mother was Native American. I remember Johnny's parents; his mother was probably Native American. I'm not sure if they picked fruit. His father was a leather tooler; he crafted folk art of Catholic themes that he and Johnny's mother sold at county fairs around rural parts of Northern California. We visited them once, when I was a child, in Oroville, where they were living. I remember his father's hands, huge and stained from leather tannins, and I can still picture the inside of the house—my mother says it was a small trailer—which was filled with leather-working tools.

Johnny, the son of these people who might be considered a certain creative underclass from the "old, weird America," was himself deeply talented, and Rattray knew it and was drawn to Johnny for something in him that was a whole lot freer than anything in Rattray. Johnny was not escaping anything. He was into the honeypot of life as a natural disposition, whether living on the banks of a river, fishing and eating pilfered orchard fruits, or committing to no posterity whatsoever his "action poetry," which took the form, for instance, of pissing on someone's brand-new Cadillac, parked on the streets of downtown St. Louis. (Another action poem: before entering a Goodwill thrift shop with my mother, Johnny placed his partly smoked joint on the hood of a car. As they left, he picked it up and continued to smoke it, brazen behavior for the early 1960s, when possession could land you ten years in prison—a place Johnny already knew well.)

Alden and Johnny were both kindred enjoyers of life. Alden, as Rattray describes him, saunters into a Mexican bordello "as if he owns the place." Rattray's admiration is not just that Alden can play it cool but that for Alden, as he tells Rattray, the kingdom of heaven is "on earth" and "no place else." In a bordello, at a gas station, or at the soft-serve window. On an outing to a carnival freak show, Rattray marvels at Johnny's ability to "fall in with carny talk and point of view." Rattray is watching people who possess a talent for life, people who are not seekers of the invisible but embodied creatures whose life *is* the poem, not split off from, in Alden's case, the poetry he writes.

Rattray was not only formally educated and intensely cerebral— fluent in French, German, Latin, and ancient Greek—he seems to have been someone for whom the world was full of mystery but like a book is full of mysteries, as if the world *were itself a book*, one that was crammed with tiny, secret writings. And the way to understand that book—this world—was to diligently decode it. Throughout *How I Became*, Rattray interprets people through lines of poetry: Swinburne, Keats, Stefan George, Beckett. When he encounters Pound in person, he interprets Pound through lines of Pound.

In "Van," Alden tells Rattray that his "European esthetic standards" don't apply to "the reality of America." They argue, and Rattray leaves the Bay Area, where Alden has gone to seek a miracle cure to his illness. Rattray hitchhikes to St. Louis and moves in with Johnny Sherrill, as if his failure to connect to one idol, or ideal, produces in him the commitment to do so with the other.

For Rattray, invisibility meant to take leave of the self in order to merge, or submerge, into life, to finally understand it. Some don't crave that kind of understanding. Don't need it. They are in the water, and not only do they resist interpreting the water, they don't even call it "water." Johnny, in particular, was not decoding people or decodable, and instead taking his share, whether he had to poach it or grift it or earn it, or whether it simply fell in his lap. When he and Rattray outrun the police and end up at the home of a drunk whose wife pours their bag of fried pigs' snouts into a serving bowl, the environment, this woman, her tired resignation, the plastic on all the furniture in the place, are notable to Rattray, and recorded beautifully, but *foreign*. Johnny is his emissary into streams of American life. And the first instance of Rattray's transition to what he calls invisibility takes place while standing watch over the wild marijuana he and Johnny are attempting to harvest along a river bottom outside Kansas City. As if what Rattray called invisibility was pursued under Johnny's aegis.

In the years just before I was born, my mother and father lived in North St. Louis, near Johnny and his common-law wife, Freddie. After my parents left St. Louis in a converted school bus that Johnny convinced them to buy, to move to Oregon, we returned to St. Louis in the summers, which was how I got to know Freddie Sherrill and the world of North St. Louis's Labadie Avenue, which Rattray portrays in his book. I remember Johnny and Freddie's son Gary and my brother setting off fireworks on summer nights, and no one in that neighborhood minding. My mother tells of a Fourth of July when Johnny shot his gun out the door in a celebratory impulse, but forgot to open the screen and put a hole in it. Freddie's father, Daddy Quinn, was a preacher who addressed a congregation that wasn't visible to the rest of us. He preached to the rows of empty automobile bench seats that he'd arranged in the side yard of the family's house. I remember understanding that Daddy Quinn's quirks were allowed, as if his family, and the people around those parts, let him be who he was. No one said anything. It was all dealt with incredibly gently. Around the old car seats were crosses nailed to all the trees, to keep evil spirits away. Daddy Quinn had speakers mounted on the bumpers of his truck, and he drove up and down Labadie Avenue preaching the amplified word to people gathered on their stoops, to the air, to whomever. I remember hearing him from inside the house, which was always very dark—perhaps people were careful not to waste electricity, or maybe it was shut off, I'm not sure—as I sat in the parlor with Freddie's mother, Ma Dear, and a bunch of other relatives, eating White Castle hamburgers. I had been told by my parents that White Castle was racist and that we didn't eat their burgers on account of it. But there I was in a house full of black people enjoying them.

These are things you remember. Lessons you draw, even if you never find out what the lesson was. Freddie's great-grandmother, who also lived in the house, had been born, as Rattray points out, before the Civil War had ended. She must have been almost 110 years old when I knew her.

Rattray identifies the women in that world as prostitutes, but like Johnny's pimping, this is another balloon my mother pricks, but differently, explaining that it wasn't a label you would use for anyone in North St. Louis, but rather a realm in which many women, by necessity, supplemented their income. Women weren't prostitutes as an identity; they were practical and knew how to survive.

While she was still young and beautiful, Freddie Sherrill died of a heart attack. The house on Labadie Avenue was burned down by a wayward grandchild who knocked wanting money from Ma Dear and was refused entry. Many of the housing lots in North St. Louis have returned to the prairie, leaving soft grasses and crumbling traces of foundation. Long before this, Johnny had drifted west, worked as a machinist up in Washington State. Later he worked in the shipyards in San Francisco, where he showed off to us the leather patchwork "pimp coat" he'd made for himself by hand. Did Johnny know that Rattray, whom Johnny once introduced to his parole officer as an instructor at Harvard, would later immortalize him as an *actual* pimp? Johnny was an unclassifiable character—perhaps ultimately unreadable to anyone who might be believably presented to a parole officer as a Harvard instructor. (Rattray was doing graduate studies there. Nevertheless, the officer told Johnny that Rattray looked "mighty strange.")

When Johnny catches a fish in the shallows where he and Rattray are harvesting marijuana, he says to the fish, "Aren't you a deep goodie." This is pure Johnny and I can hear him say it. And the situations Rattray describes are pure Johnny: picking up, by accident, an outlaw hitchhiker who had just murdered his family, and introducing Alden to the Harlem Club across the Mississippi, in East St. Louis, where Alden is seduced by a transgender beauty. My father tells a story of a night out with Johnny at the Harlem Club, when the couple in the next booth over, a dapper and quite elderly black gentleman and a nubile teenage girl, white, obviously working as an escort, asked the club photographer to take their picture for hire. (The Harlem Club was notably a place that did not discriminate against interracial couples.) Just before the flashbulb went off, Johnny turned around and put his head between this couple. Photobombing avant la lettre. The photo was developed on-site and delivered to the couple in their booth. The girl was very pleased and proud, even despite Johnny's ghostly face between her and her date.

The Harlem Club, which was just beyond a stockyard and right up against the railroad tracks, had a giant neon sign of a waiter holding a cocktail. In 1967, my parents went back to the site of the club. It had been demolished earlier that year. On the ground, my father found a piece of its famous neon sign and picked it up. He still has it somewhere. I'd like to see it, but will this fragment tell me about the Harlem Club? Certainly not.

FLYING CARS

Every time I've tried to start this side-winding meditation on art-ist Matthew Porter's airborne muscle cars, cars that are things and also backlit silhouettes of things, I end up scrolling *Autotrader* online, and looking at models of cars I've always wanted and haven't yet owned, and also their silhouettes.

If I had a hundred grand to drop right now, this morning, which I don't, I could buy a 1969 GTO Judge, mint. But really it's not my style. A '67 GTO and its classy cigar-box lines are what I always wanted. The '69 is a novelty item, like roller skates or a leather shirt, and anyhow I would get bored of the color orange. I'd love a GTO but I don't need a Judge, even if there are certain days—Tuesdays?—when I feel like I do need a Judge.

For a Sunday drive I want a Stutz Blackhawk; doesn't even have to be the one Elvis owned. I will humbly accept some other Stutz, but the more I research who owned Stutzes—Dean Martin, Wilson Pickett, George Foreman, Muhammad Ali, Willie Nelson, and Barry White, just to cherry-pick from the longer list of celebrity owners— I get mad that I haven't yet myself acquired the pink slip for a Stutz. Even if I could afford one, there aren't very many, and today none are listed for sale.

There's a 1965 Mercury Marauder. I always liked those. Even if the lines are a little square, the fastback makes up for it, but it's a car that has to have sport rims or forget it.

Why is 1965 the chicane through which all American car design went from curved to boxy?

Nineteen sixty-eight was another chicane, which led to puffy quarter panels, and even outright blimpage.

Sometimes I start to believe I want a Rolls-Royce, like a model from the 1980s, which can occasionally be a bargain. Andy Warhol owned a 1974 Silver Shadow in chocolate brown. He told his boyfriend, Jed Johnson, to lie and say that Andy traded the car for art instead of purchased it at the dealer. Andy didn't drive, and was instead chauffered by Johnson, or, on occasion, by Imelda Marcos. Recently, that Rolls originally owned by Warhol was for sale on eBay, though I don't know the final bid. Today you can buy a 1985 Rolls-Royce Silver Spur for a mere ten grand on *Autotrader*. I know nothing about Rolls models, but if it doesn't come with pull-down teakwood dinner trays in the back seat, the deal is off. Extras are important to me. The idea of a General Motors Lanvin Arpège perfume atomizer offered stock with the 1958 Cadillac Eldorado Brougham spritzes my spirit with something American that I can actually, for a moment, believe in.

I often desire a 1961 Ford Starliner. That's something special to me, and it harkens back to one I saw for sale in Napa, California, in 1992. It was Wimbledon White, a stock Ford color I'm partial to. I still regret that I didn't buy it. Say it: *Starliner*. Say *Wimbledon White*. That was the year I spent every weekend looking at cars. I ended up buying a 1964 Ford Galaxie, which I still own, but even after I bought my Galaxie I continued combing *PennySaver* and *Autotrader* and *Hemmings* and called telephone numbers and dreamed of other cars. In 1997, I bought a 1963 Chevrolet Impala in Hendersonville, North Carolina. The night I bought it, a friend and I motored out to a drive-in movie theater in

Waynesville. We could hear cows lowing as we waited for the film to begin. I wish I still had that car. I had to sell it to pay living expenses, made a large profit since it's a coveted year of a coveted model. The night before I sold it, someone attempted to steal it from my parents' driveway in San Francisco. My neighbor saw my car in the middle of the street and knocked on our door. A guy had hot-wired it and was planning to drive away with the anti-theft Club still attached to the wheel. He flooded the engine trying to give it gas and had to abandon my car on foot.

It's September as I write this, and the 2018 calendar my son got at the Pomona Car Show is turned to a 1971 Mustang Boss 351. I've seen every muscle car a hundred times over. That was youth. This is now (middle age). I've given my copy of the *Standard Catalog of American Cars, 1946–1975* to my son, who pores over specs like I once did. (He thought my Galaxie was cool until he learned that it also came stock from the factory with a 427 big block, and asked why I have a mere 289. I defensively argued mine handles better with less weight on the front end but he wasn't fully convinced.)

The '71 Mustang on the car show calendar is parked in front of a tacky Italianate villa. The parked car is object instead of subject. The cars photographed by Matthew Porter and digitally manipulated to look as if flying through intersections are protagonists; that's clear. A midair car knows the story and it is the story, even if the casual grace of electric wires, light poles, and traffic signals plays its part. Twilight puts the city-sky infrastructure into relief: the light is half the charm of these magical images. The locations that Porter has chosen, too, are sweet, but maybe in part because they're familiar: some of them are in my neighborhood, or near it. He doesn't photograph famously steep

Baxter Street in Echo Park, but his images conjure it. Cresting Baxter to get air is something LAPD motorcycle cops do at five a.m., when they figure no one is paying attention. They hit Baxter Street and court broken axles.

There are many iconic cinema stills of flying muscle cars, but the mother lode of the genre is from H. B. Halicki's 1974 film *Gone in 60 Seconds*, in which a Mustang Mach 1 hovers midair in a Los Angeles intersection after launching off a crash pile it has used as a jump ramp.

The film's superflimsy plotline involves the theft of forty-eight cars in forty-eight hours, each coded with a woman's name. The Mach 1, called Eleanor, is the indisputable star of the movie and credited as such. Halicki financed, produced, directed, wrote, starred in, and did all of the stunt driving for this film. He was known as the Car Crash King, and he was also the Junkyard King, who owned all ninety-three of the vehicles that were totaled in his movie, including multiple police cars and fire trucks. Even the garbage truck that drives right over a Dodge Charger is from Halicki's personal collection. In my favorite scene, Eleanor the Mach 1 plows into a large sofa that's sitting in the middle of an alleyway, the cushions compressed and pulverized as the car commits to dragging the ruined frame of the couch from its undercarriage for several hundred feet.

There are other comic touches. Halicki evades police in a tow truck with a rear-facing Dodge Challenger, a mint car that later gets shoved in a compactor at a wrecking yard. Cornered at one point after a high-speed pursuit in the Mach 1, Halicki seems to assent to the police, as if the game is over. He puts his hands up at officers' commands, multiple guns drawn on him from various angles. He keeps his hands up, but mashes the gas with his driving foot, complying and not complying, hands kept up as he blazes west on Ocean Boulevard in Long Beach and cops dive out of the way. This has become a metaphor at our house, where you pay lip service to some bullshit enforcer, put your hands up, but mash the gas.

In other highlights, Eleanor the Mach 1 runs over a shopping cart full of groceries. A night scene at the long-gone Ascot Park speedway reveals the inspiration for the film's title, a message for speedway guests to lock their vehicles or they'll be "gone in sixty seconds." A high-speed chase interrupts the Carson City Council's dedication of a new sheriff's department, a scene I favor because Carson is where, coincidentally, the best go-karting in Los Angeles can be had—or rather, the most scrappy and sketchy go-karting in Los Angeles can be had. Another highlight is when Eleanor drives right into a Cadillac dealership, escaping through the service department.

But the heart of the film is a long and static sequence in a huge garage, as the camera slow-pans past every one of the forty-eight stolen vehicles, Rolls-Royces and Cadillacs and Lincolns, a Plymouth Barracuda, a Corvette Stingray, a Manta Mirage, car after car, some rare, some not, all gleaming and still. They are part of the contrived and made-up plot, but the cars are real—actual vehicles that belonged to an actual Halicki (and which, in real life, he'd acquired dubiously). A woman named Pumpkin sits behind a desk, the superego in the room, leaning back. She has big hair—I mean really big, amazing hair—and long nails. The studs on the collar of her denim shirt wink at the camera, her Malibu-tan hands tented in rumination, although maybe she's thinking only of money, or of nothing at all. Either way, I love her. Her real name is not Pumpkin but Marion Busia, and apparently she is now, according to Google, a real estate agent in Rancho Palos Verdes. I'd settle for nothing less.

Joined to the theme of destroying cars is a fetish for cars, but fetishes also for other kinds of stuff. Halicki wears a different belt buckle in every scene, and none are subtle. He's got a lot of sunglasses, bell-bottoms, and briefcases. Several wigs and an artificial mustache. Various styles of slim jim, for opening car doors. An array of hats and deerskin driving gloves. Halicki was a collector. I heard he later acquired his own Goodyear Blimp, but I'm having trouble verifying that.

Halicki died while filming a sequel to *Gone in 60 Seconds*. A telephone pole was clipped by a wire meant to pull a water tower into a parking lot full of cars, and the telephone pole hit Halicki and killed him.

Time passes. People become real estate agents. People die. Car collections get auctioned. Classics become more valuable, and rarer, and also forgotten, and thus, to some, less valuable, and that's good, and also sad.

The light stays the same. Or rather, it is always changing.

PICTURE·BOOK HORSES

owdy, partner. I promise you no one says that in the 1,056 pages of *The Border Trilogy*, which feature the tribulations of some rather existential cowboys. All in all, Cormac McCarthy's vaqueros don't say much, but they especially don't talk in horsey clichés. Neither do they talk like people usually do in novels, by which I mean the type of novels popularized in the nineteenth century and still for some mysterious reason going strong today. While other people in other books psychologize and divulge, these people, in these semi-linked books, are busy silently resisting rudimentary and wholly external forces: terrain and weather and enemies. Their needs are for clothing and food and water and shelter, and for safety both from malevolence and from natural and impersonal forms of danger. They need boots. They need rifles. Saddle blankets and canteens.

For a long time I didn't like Western films as a genre, because they were boring to me without any women. With Sam Peckinpah, I yawned and waited to glimpse the ladies in the saloon or on the train platform. They appear only rarely. Nicholas Ray was an exception. *Johnny Guitar* was an exception. But the icy virago in that film, played by Joan Crawford, was also the exception, so it all kind of cancels itself out. Strangely, I didn't take much issue with the relative lack of women in *The Border Trilogy*, having read the books eagerly, one by one, as they emerged over the course of the 1990s: *All the Pretty Horses* (1992), *The Crossing* (1994), and *Cities of the Plain* (1998). And various women do appear, such as Dueña Alfonsa, who offers to John Grady a pessimistic worldview that is the strongest statement in *All the Pretty Horses*. But generally speaking the women say even less than the cowboys and we never enter their thoughts. What I realized, in rereading these books, is that I had adopted, naturally, the points of view of the male characters, because that is where, in the books, subjectivity lies. Even if the men don't reveal much interiority, we take their perspective as they struggle, and struggle in these books is the essential condition of life.

John Grady wants to locate a world he can recognize as historically continuous. In *The Crossing*, Billy Parham wants to return a wolf that he has captured and muzzled to the mountains of Mexico. In addition perhaps Billy Parham wants to enter into mythological time, approach something like a set of eternal laws. That these desires are not justified in conventional passages of interiority is part of the unique artistic vision of Cormac McCarthy. No purpose is ever stated.

We know only predicament, but the predicament is loaded. John Grady's, and Billy's, too, is something like that of the mercenaries in Xenophon's *Anabasis*, who lose their leader and in a sense their war, and find themselves wandering in an alien land. Even when lost, McCarthy's cowboys don't doubt or hope or suspect or wonder. Instead they are defined by know-how, as Heidegger might put it. They roll their own and strike anywhere, but mostly off a thumbnail. They rope and break wild horses. And the reader too acquires skills, such as reading beautifully worked prose that has no commas. They go without beds. We go without commas and feel liberated.

The reader, like these cowboys, will eventually acclimate to the landscape as a totalizing reality, where meditation and resistance are two components of one realm, a destiny of wandering the borderlands of the United States and Mexico in the postwar twentieth century.

At the beginning of *All the Pretty Horses*, John Grady's family is about to sell their ranch and end a multi-generation-long tradition. He's sixteen when he and his friend Lacey Rawlins set out for Mexico, in search of something like authenticity, or at least adventure. Prairie women don't provide home-cooked vittles for their big send-off. The boys stop and buy supplies that are packed into a number-four grocery bag. But the ironies McCarthy layers in don't rely on crude dichotomies in regard to historical transformation. The postwar twentieth-century frontier, where cowboys purchase groceries, is not the corruption of some pure origin. The origin is understood to be itself a corruption. An oil painting in the dining room of the Grady Family ranch features horses breaking through a pole corral. When John Grady asks his grandfather what breed they are, "his grandfather looked up from his plate at the painting as if he'd never seen it before and he said those are picturebook horses and went on eating."

Picture-book horses in a picture-book West are part of the historical record, a history that "seethes on . . . well into the third millennium," as Harold Bloom wrote, referring to the events depicted in McCarthy's *Blood Meridian* (1985). If that novel precedes *The Border Trilogy* both chronologically and by its historical content, the same stretch and reach of colonial conquest and war inform all four novels, with *Blood Meridian* as the primal scene of extreme violence in the borderlands of Texas and Mexico in 1849. The facts of history, that paramilitary forces were sent to murder as many Indians as possible, and the mystification of history—with its picture-book horses and its John Waynes—are profoundly woven into the trilogy that came next. Nominally Westerns, these books are too entropic and philosophical to fit within the limits of the genre. They summon the ghosts of history, and haunt the gaps between justice and reality.

As I revisited the trilogy recently, I was in a home office that is walking distance from the largest bas-relief military monument in the United States, celebrating the 1847 victory of Los Angeles in the Mexican-American War. This enormous terra-cotta bas relief of a battalion of soldiers, one on horseback, and the rippling American flag they raise, lies diagonal from the huge criminal court building in downtown Los Angeles. Mexican Americans stream past this monument celebrating Mexico's defeat, dwarfed by its fifty-foot height, as they make their way to court, where disproportionate numbers of Latinos are arraigned, tried, convicted, and remanded to state prisons.

Which is to say that history seethes onward indeed. John Grady's attempt to find the authentic way to live his destiny, be a man in the West—by going to Mexico—is itself tinged with ironies. Until he and Lacey Rawlins reach the border, they are traveling from fence to fence, in a land bounded and defined by private property. On the rare occasion they need and use money, their commerce seems primitive, reluctant, although they do occasionally enjoy a heavy ceramic plate of diner food, in scenes that could almost be cut from the cinematic cloth of *Hud* or *The Last Picture Show*—both of which, like *The Border Trilogy*, take place in the twilight of Western ranching.

When John Grady reaches the Rio Grande, he crosses naked (to keep his clothes dry), and the symbolism of his Adamic rebirth into Mexico is obvious. McCarthy understands the myth of the American Adam and the American Eden. Adam does not spring from nowhere. In this case he comes from Texas. And he will return north and reappear in book three to witness the transformation of the West into a staging ground for nuclear annihilation. He and Billy Parham both travel back and forth, variously, over the panoramic stretch of three books. They are homesteaders of the body, not the land. But even the American myth of self-reliance and, further, of selfhood, is pulverized artfully by McCarthy, who seems to want to dismantle not only the myth of the new world and its new man, but the myth of novelistic truth.

If both the ideological plague and central mission of the novel as an art form have been to reveal the interiority of individual lives, McCarthy has loosed his characters of all that. When John Grady, at the end of *All the Pretty Horses*, "passed and paled into the darkening land, the world to come," he joins with both the living world and the engulfing landscape. He pales. He fades away. And even if he does eventually return in book three, we are left at the end of the first book with a majestic idea of the absolution of self: John Grady goes to Mexico a teenage boy and returns north a figure literally merging with the void. How he feels matters not at all.

This is one of my favorite moments in literature. If the choice of "pale" by a writer with great range and control is not incidental, then we must take the rider in the scene to be the fourth horseman of the apocalypse, who rides the pale horse. Like a slow-acting hallucinogen, the book has managed to transform a Texas boy of sixteen looking for adventure into a mysterious image that augurs the destruction of the world. He is no longer John Grady. He is Death.

NOT WITH THE BAND

The legendary Bay Area concert promoter Bill Graham was gone by the time I came to work for his company in 1993, but it didn't feel that way. Everyone talked about Bill Graham in the present tense. Bill Graham Presents managed the Fillmore theater on Geary Boulevard and the Warfield on Market Street, both gorgeous old-school San Francisco live-music venues where I tended bar in my early and mid-twenties and saw hundreds of musicians perform. "I work for Bill Graham," we staffers all said, but Bill Graham was dead, killed in a helicopter crash in 1991.

While I was growing up in San Francisco, his name was attached to everything to do with rock and roll; all the big concerts were Bill Graham events. I had seen Graham up close only once. My friends and I were trying to sneak into a Clash concert at the Civic Auditorium downtown. It was 1984. I had just turned fifteen. I was with another girl my age and some older guys from the Sunset District, the not-chic neighborhood where we all lived. To put it bluntly, we were ratty delinquents looking for beer, weed, and opportunities for theft and trespass. Our methods for getting into concerts, occasionally effective, were to rush emergency side doors and run for it, disappearing into the crowd so that security could not find us and drag us out. We were lurking outside the Civic Auditorium when the Clash started their set, with "London Calling." One of the older guys, named Ray, tried to kick in a set of doors in his steel-toed boots, but the doors had a chain securing them. He was kicking repeatedly to bust the chain when I heard a roar. A person who looked homeless came charging at Ray, knocking him down, and Ray and this wild creature went tumbling and struggling into the bushes, wrestling each other. What was happening seemed no longer about us getting into the Clash concert. It was some kind of personal beef between our friend and this crazed man, who, it turned out, was not actually a homeless person. It was Bill Graham.

I don't know if Graham enjoyed fistfights, or if he felt he had to take it upon himself to personally secure this large venue (now named after him, posthumously), or maybe both, but later I learned he was notorious for brawls like this one.

We didn't get inside to see the Clash that night, but I'd seen the Clash before, when they toured with the Who in 1982. I was fourteen and had spent the night with two other girlfriends on a sidewalk outside the Oakland Coliseum, in order to position ourselves close to the stage when they started letting people into the stadium the next morning. We had sleeping bags but didn't sleep; we partied with strangers, which is what I spent a lot of my youth doing. Just before the stadium entrances opened, an adult shared a joint with me and my friends. The joint was laced with PCP, and by the time the line started moving, I was stunned and wandering.

A lot of the concerts of my youth were scary like that, but also exciting, on account of the menace they promised. Like Black Sabbath at the Cow Palace in Daly City, when I was about twelve. I was in awe of these roving groups of older teenage girls who were all wearing tight bell-bottom jeans with an exposed zipper down the front, and then up the back—as if the pants, or maybe these girls, were held together entirely by this zipper that vertically bisected and looped their pelvises. The parking lot scene of the Black Sabbath concert, as I remember it, looked like Géricault's painting of the half-dead shipwreck survivors on the raft of the *Medusa*, but with long-haired shirtless guys in boot-cut Levi's passed out or throwing up next to someone's van.

That year I somehow ended up at a Sammy Hagar concert, judge as you will. A painted portrait of Sammy Hagar with his famous red guitar was passed overhand by the crowd from the back of the Cow Palace to the stage, where Sammy Hagar accepted it to thundering applause. He placed the painting on his guitar stand like it was an easel. I can still see that painting, if not the dumpster where it probably ended up.

My very first concert had been the Rolling Stones, on their *Tattoo You* tour, at Candlestick Park. I went with my older brother. We got to go because our mother, while walking to work one morning, decided to get in line with the group gathered outside the Record Factory when she learned that everyone was waiting to get Stones tickets. I remember that the Stones were late going onstage. In his memoir, Bill Graham recounts why: the heel on Keith Richards's boot broke off, and Keith was superstitious about wearing the right boots and refused to play unless the heel could be fixed. Bill Graham ran around until he found someone with a heel like on Keith's boot, begged the owner for the shoe, offering one hundred dollars in exchange, tore the heel off the sole and hobnailed it to Keith's old boot, yelling and swearing the whole time.

My first record, as a child, was Blondie's *Parallel Lines*, which I bought with my paper route money when I was nine. I concentrated so hard on the photograph on the cover, of Debbie Harry in her cream-colored slip-dress and self-styled "militant" armband, her matching high-heeled Candie's, that I can still make my heart ache with the yearning I felt, which was not for her but to be her. I thought my own far-off adolescence was going to manifest as a result of the hard work of concentrating on beauty as if it were a vanishing point. The soundtrack of anticipation, of this ardent waiting, was every song on *Parallel Lines*.

In college, at UC Berkeley, I worked underage with a fake ID as a cocktail waitress at a nightclub on Shattuck Avenue called the Til Two Lounge, where Bay Area soul and blues legends performed live. It was an entire world, inside this shabby place that reeked of empty kegs and stale smoke. The owner, Nat Bolden, sometimes stepped from behind the bar, took the mic and sang. He had a beautiful voice.

After college, I moved back to San Francisco and got a job serving drinks at a dive bar called the Blue Lamp, on Geary and Jones, at the top of the Tenderloin. The Blue Lamp featured live music at night, a mix of punk, torch singers, and rock bands. On Sunday afternoons there was a raucous and fairly terrible blues jam that was an entertaining gallery of personalities, with an eccentric band leader who once, while I was bartending, ran into the street, soloing in the pouring rain on his electric guitar, which allowed for freedom of movement because it was cordless. He shocked the hell out of himself in the rain. On weekday afternoons, the Blue Lamp was quiet except for the old drunks who sat at the bar. One of them, a regular, used to tell me he thought I could "do better" with my life. He would assess me physically as he said it, as if his approval of my looks was a sign that I might manage to avoid complete ruin. He was condescending, while I thought it was me who had the upper hand over him, since he was just an old Tenderloin bum who didn't know I was an actual college graduate and aspiring writer. But if I admitted that to him, I would seem like a level of loser he hadn't even contemplated: an educated person, working in a dump!

*   *   *

I don't remember how I got my job at the Warfield, but it felt like a triumphant step upward. The Warfield was a glamorous old theater with an elaborate movie palace interior, grand antebellum-style stairwells, and enormous chandeliers. Everyone from Neil Young to PJ Harvey to Iggy Pop played there. Each evening was different at the Warfield, the mood created by the scheduled performer and their crowd, and whether or not the show was a sold-out affair.

If it was someone like Sonic Youth, we were there not just to make money but to see a great show. If it was Jerry Garcia, it was pure work, a meal ticket, since the Jerry Garcia Band performed at the Warfield scores of nights each year, and their crowd bought a lot of drinks. We made good money at their shows, but we employees were in a war with their patrons, the Deadheads, who set up encampments out front on Market Street, left their garbage everywhere, and didn't respect us or pay attention to rules. They routinely spilled beer, vomited on the velvet seats in the theater, trashed the restrooms. If you reprimanded them, they'd tell you to "mellow" or "be cool."

We didn't just hate them because they were hippies but because a lot of them seemed like rich kids who had never had to work. We sometimes retaliated by shortchanging them. If they were wasted and handed over a twenty-dollar bill for a draft beer, we'd hand them arbitrary change, a couple of dollars, some coins, and keep the rest. At the time, it seemed like a fair tax. I never interacted with Jerry, but his backstage meal service requests were infamous, including dishes like scallops wrapped in bacon with a ready fondue pot for dipping them. Surprisingly, this diet was not the cause of his death. Instead, it was the mixture of heroin and cocaine he favored. He would get so high during the break between sets that on at least one occasion paramedics were called, and Jerry was revived before the band came back onstage to play their second set.

The load-in crew had their own stories about performers and bands.

For instance Glenn Danzig toured with an extra eighteen-wheeler that was for transporting his mobile weight-lifting gym. When the Allman Brothers played a string of performances, each night we were on standby to find out if the show was actually happening, because, as we were told, Dickey Betts might not be able to play. He was having personal struggles of some kind—imagine what you will—and yet Dickey, the most notorious one, has outlived the rest.

When the blues legend Buddy Guy played the Warfield, in a moment that echoed the Blue Lamp bandleader running out to solo in the rain, Buddy Guy jumped from the stage and came up the aisle to the bar I was manning, and stopped playing to ask for a Heineken. I handed it to him, and he downed it and went back to playing.

One regular theater patron was Carlos Santana, who was friends with the managers and got to come in free. We were instructed to comp all his drinks. He was like a guy dressed up as Carlos Santana, with the mustache and the shallow-brimmed black fedora pulled down over his eyes. He always ordered Cuervo, neat, and he never left a tip—not even a dollar!

All of us employees were friends—the bartenders, cocktail waitresses, food servers, cooks, security, and stage crews. At the end of the night, we were allowed to stay for close-out, post-work drinks, when the theater was emptied of patrons. It was like a mating ritual, as everyone at the Warfield dated one another. I remember being told that while the rest of us were hanging out in the lobby, the general operations manager left through a side exit with a metal briefcase handcuffed to his wrist, the protocol for stashing the cash from a night's take.

We were sometimes sent to bartend special off-site Bill Graham events, like a rare performance at the Oakland Paramount by Tom Waits that was a legal defense fundraiser for a friend of his awaiting trial. Tom Waits started talking to people in the audience as if they were old friends, and I understood immediately that it was improvised poetry. "You still workin' out at the airport?" he asked a guy in the front row. And to another, "How many scorpions did you have to shake from those boots before you put them on?"

On the opposite end of the spectrum was a soulless event we worked for a company party at a giant stadium somewhere in the South Bay. It was a private concert given by Rod Stewart for the employees of whatever company it was (I don't recall). We had to wear ugly polo shirts and khakis, and everyone was making fun of one another in these sad outfits. We served, at that event, four types of drink: Bud Light, Bud Dry, regular Budweiser, and some other Bud derivation. Attendees at this corporate event mulled the options like they were actual choices. "Hmm. So hard to decide. How about . . . a Bud Light?" Rod Stewart came out and preened and whooped like this wasn't just some hellish money gig for him. The crowd loved it. Don't want to give raises and benefits? Hire Rod Stewart once a year, and serve Bud Light.

When the historic Fillmore theater reopened in keeping with a long-held wish of the late Bill Graham, we all got to work there too. The Fillmore was an elegant Italianate theater that was built as a dance hall in 1910. It had suffered structural damage in the 1989 earthquake and was repaired and reopened in 1994 with a secret show by the Smashing Pumpkins, which sold out in less than a minute. After the show, a stagehand gave me a pale blue guitar pick that had been left on an amp by James Iha, whom I had a crush on. I probably still have that pick, even if the Smashing Pumpkins have not endured and it isn't music I'd ever listen to again.

The Fillmore is a smaller theater than the Warfield; the environment is more intimate, and also keyed up, if the performer is someone really famous, because the audience is so close to them. I often worked at the bar that was facing the stage, so I had a great view of the show. Johnny Cash opened his Fillmore set with "Folsom Prison Blues" and later asked the crowd if they'd mind if he brought a special guest, June Carter Cash, and everyone went crazy. Nick Cave and the Bad Seeds arranged with our sound people to have a Barry White song play before they went on. As "I'm Gonna Love You Just a Little Bit More Baby" filled the theater, the drummer of the Bad Seeds sat down at his kit. He started tapping his high-hat cymbal in beat to this Barry White song. One by one the musicians came onstage and joined in. In a sharkskin suit and white shoes, Nick Cave took the microphone, and the transition from Barry White to the Bad Seeds was complete.

Courtney Love's band Hole played the Fillmore seven or eight months after Kurt Cobain died. His death still felt raw. Love came onstage and pointed out people in the crowd whom she'd dated or had bad sex with and described their various faults into the microphone. Mid-set, she stopped playing, looked up at the lighting rack over the stage as if at heaven, creating an awkward tension in the crowd, which was silent. She screamed, "COME BACK!" The response was raised eyebrows and shrugs: no one seemed moved by her theatrics.

A main ambition at that time in my life was to look as glamorous as the environments I worked in, or my interpretation of glamour—this was the nineties—which meant vintage clothes mostly in velvet or silver Lurex knits or leather. The Warfield theater manager was constantly on my case for my outfits, which she felt were inappropriate. Exposed midriffs were her special bête noire, but she found a way to shame me for whatever I wore. "I don't ever need to see you naked," she once said to me, "because *those pants* give me all the information." We all made fun of her and the bar manager for being company stooges. The bar manager was the sort of person who shaved his head with hot water and a straight razor because that method, he said, was "more honest." When Brian Setzer played one New Year's, he gave me the once-over and invited me downstairs (backstage) after the show. The bar manager saw the exchange and told me if I went downstairs to hang out with Brian Setzer I'd be fired. I'm still mad about that, even if Brian Setzer was slightly old for my taste. These managers were killjoys, but that's a manager's lot.

Which was why it was so curious that we all got calls one day about a secret, private Halloween party we were requested to work, and the evening required "outrageous costumes: anything goes." The theater manager even called me and bitchily said, "Go ahead and dress like a slut."

It's hard to keep secrets at a theater with a huge staff, and yet none of us knew whom this party was for until after we got there. The Warfield had been transformed into what looked like a surrealist film set, with purple gels over all the lights, fountains and waterways of floating gardenias, and the loge of the theater filled with silver and black balloons.

The party was for the Rolling Stones, who were on tour. Or rather, the party was being given *by* the Rolling Stones, as a way to thank their road crew. Apparently it was a tradition of theirs that each member of the band would work, serving drinks to their crew. Each of us bartenders was paired with one member of the band as our work partner. Reader, I was paired with Keith Richards. He was in keeping with the legends: drank Jack and gingers all night long, personally draining probably two bottles of Jack Daniel's. He and the band's business manager had to be kicked out of the theater at dawn by security guards, the two of them the hardest-partying attendees of the night.

Mick Jagger was also in keeping with legends, at least the recent legends: he wore an ascot, drank Evian, and left before midnight with a socialite from Mill Valley. The rest of the band served their crew and took turns jamming onstage with a whole host of Bay Area musicians who were invited to play. I ran into people at that party I hadn't seen in years, like childhood friend Arion Salazar, who was the bassist in the band Third Eye Blind. Imagine what he must have felt: he jammed with the Stones that night!

I started picking up shifts at another venue, the Great American Music Hall on O'Farrell. It was built as a bordello in 1907, and the interior was French rococo. Everyone who worked there was convinced the place was haunted. Duke Ellington had been a regular performer and his name was still on a dressing room door. The bar manager's father had worked for Van Morrison. This manager once told me a story about Van Morrison being invited to a party given in his honor, after his gig. He showed up very late, in the rain, was mistaken for a hobo, and not invited in. This seemed right to me. To make the art, and disappoint those who want to put you in their limelight.

In the summer of 1995, I was on a road trip with a friend who worked with me at the Warfield and Fillmore. We were in my '64 Ford Galaxie, at a stoplight in Jackson, Mississippi, when two guys in a pickup truck rolled up next to us and shouted, "Hey, California! Jerry Garcia died today!" I guess they thought two chicks in a classic with California plates would want to hear this breaking news. We both burst out laughing. I blame our coldhearted disaffection on the unhealthy dynamic of a workplace: we were subjected to Jerry's fans,

and so our feelings were at best very mixed about the whole phenomenon of him and his music.

And yet Jerry's death did mark a change for me, by coincidence, or
not. I was feeling, that summer, trapped into bartending, which pays
well and trains a person for exactly nothing else, and I wanted to leave
small and provincial San Francisco, move to New York City, try for
real to become a writer. I started formulating plans.

A month after Jerry died, PJ Harvey played two sold-out shows at the
Warfield, and after her second show she played a secret impromptu set
at the Hotel Utah, a dive bar South of Market. The show began at one
a.m., after her show at the Warfield. I don't know how I got invited but
I went. The Hotel Utah was a tiny room—it fit maybe forty people and
about half those there that night were band members and other musicians who took turns onstage, sitting in. PJ Harvey played all night. I
think I left at about five a.m., and she was still playing. She did not get
tired, and she did not look tired. She looked joyous, like a person in a
church, filling her soul with Holy Spirit as she sang. She stopped only
to change guitars, and the entire time, she had this otherworldly glow.
I was witness to an artist who wanted to play all night because she was
born to do it. She had passion, talent, and incredible technical skills.
She sang and played guitar for hours and hours, in an intimate setting,
after she had performed a fully rehearsed stadium act for thousands,
that very same night. This impressed me. The message I took from it
was: to be truly good at something is the very highest joy. And by infer-
ence, I understood this: to merely witness greatness is a distant cousin,
or even not related at all.

Just after that, I quit my job and changed my life.

MADE TO BURN

The first image I pinned up, to spark inspiration for what would eventually be a novel, was of a woman with tape over her mouth. She floated above my desk with a grave, almost murderous look, war paint on her cheeks, blond braids framing her face, the braids a frolicsome countertone to her intensity. The paint on her cheeks, not frolicsome. The streaks of it, dripping down, were cold, white shards, as if her face were faceted in icicles. I didn't think much about the tape over her mouth (which is actually Band-Aids over the photograph, and not over her lips themselves). This image ended up on the jacket of *The Flamethrowers*, whose first-person narrator is a young blond woman. A creature of language, silenced.

The second image I pinned up was of Ducati engineer Fabio Taglioni standing behind a 1971 750 GT. The Ducati is in metal-flake orange, Taglioni in double-knit Brioni. I didn't have an image of a girl on a motorcycle, although the book opens with the narrator riding one in the Bonneville land speed trials. She isn't me. But her sense of the heat and the light at the Salt Flats is mine.

The young woman in war paint was from an archival document of

1970s Italy, and she symbolized for me the insurrectionary foment that overtook the country in that decade. "Autonomia" was the term for this foment, the movement of the 1970s, a loose wave of people all over Italy who came together for various reasons at various times to engage in illegality and play and to find a way to act, to build forms of togetherness in a country whose working class was impotent and whose sub-working class was fed up with work, by turns joyous and full of rage, ready to revolt, which they did. There were multiple layers, of which the most shadowy, clandestine, and violent (and paradoxically, the most visible and sensational) were the Red Brigades. The Italian seventies had seemed a logical subject for fiction, on account of the fact that I kept stumbling upon its lore. It all began when I met a mysterious and magnetic woman who didn't say much, and who, when I naively asked her what she did, what she was interested in, stared at me and said, "*Niente.*" She had been the girlfriend of a "third-wave" Red Brigades terrorist, I learned. Her "*niente*" did not mean "nothing." It meant, I don't engage in what you'd call work. Or interests. I might add that I met this woman in a house on Lake Como that was filled with someone's mother's Fascist memorabilia, busts of Mussolini, D'Annunzian slogans chiseled into marble.

Which connects to the third image I pinned up as I wrote, of two proper-looking gentlemen in a World War I–era motorized contraption, an arcane cycle and bullet-shaped sidecar. Of the pair, the man in the sidecar, if passively at the mercy of the one over the handlebars, looks more self-possessed. He looks, actually, like F. T. Marinetti. I pretended that he was, and asked myself, Why did the Futurists never actually build anything? They drew vehicles on paper. They called war the world's only hygiene. But they had no relation to engineering and factories, to machines or munitions—except that a few of them lost limbs, or lives, in the war. But so did a lot of non-Futurists.

There are two central threads to *The Flamethrowers*: Italy in 1977, the crest of the movement, and New York at that time, a period I'm old enough to have seen and which has long fascinated me, when the city had a Detroit-like feel, was drained of money and its manufacturing base, and piled up with garbage. Parts of downtown became liberated zones of abandonment, populated by artists and criminals. The blackout of 1977 has a special place in my heart—the "bad" blackout, compared to 1965, the "good" blackout, when everyone in the housing projects behaved, an event whose textures DeLillo rendered so memorably in *Underworld*.

I wanted to conjure New York as an environment of energies, sounds, sensations. Not as a backdrop, a place that could resolve into history and sociology and urbanism, but rather as an entity that could not be reduced because it had become a character, in the manner that a fully complex character in fiction isn't reducible to cause, reasons, event. I looked at a lot of photographs and other evidentiary traces of downtown New York and art of the mid-1970s. Maybe a person is a tainted magnet and nothing is by chance, but what I kept finding were nude women and guns. The group Up Against the Wall Motherfucker, which figures in the novel, papered the Lower East Side in the late 1960s with posters that said, "We're looking for people who like to draw," with an image of a revolver. I had already encountered plenty of guns in researching Italy—the more militant elements of the Autonomist movement had an official weapon, the Walther P38, which could be blithely denoted with the thumb out, pointer finger angled up. I would scan the images of rallies in Rome, a hundred thousand people, among whom a tenth, I was told by people who had been there, were armed. Ten thousand individuals on the streets of Rome with guns in their pockets.

Among New York artists, I hadn't expected guns, and yet that's what I encountered: lots of guns and, as I said, lots of nude women. Occasionally in the same image: Hannah Wilke in strappy heels holding a petite purse pistol—like Honey West, but naked. Mostly it was men posing with the guns: William Burroughs, William Eggleston, Sandro Chia, Richard Serra. Warhol's gun drawings. Chris Burden out in Los Angeles having a friend shoot him. And women with their clothes off: Carolee Schneemann, Hannah Wilke, Francesca Woodman, Ana Mendieta, Marina Abramović, who was both nude and with a loaded gun pointed at her head (by a man).

What does all this mean? Many things, I'm sure, but for starters, it means people were getting out of the studio. Art was now about acts not sellable; it was about gestures and bodies. It was freedom, a realm where a guy could shoot off his rifle. Ride his motorcycle over a dry lakebed. Put a bunch of stuff on the floor—dirt, for instance, or lumber. Drive a forklift into a museum, or a functional race car.

But that's art history. For the purposes of a novel, what did it mean? I was faced with the pleasure and headache of somehow stitching together the pistols and the nude women as defining features of a fictional realm, and one in which the female narrator, who has the last word, and technically all words, is nevertheless continually overrun, effaced, and silenced by the very masculine world of the novel she inhabits—a contradiction I had to navigate, just as I had to find a way to merge what were by nature static and iconic images into a stream of life, real narrative life.

As I wrote, events from my time, my life, began to echo those in the book, as if I were inside a game of call-and-response. While I wrote fiction about ultraleft subversives, *The Coming Insurrection*, a book written by an anonymous French collective, was published in the United States and its authors were arrested in France. As I wrote about riots, they were exploding in Greece. As I wrote about looting, it was rampant in London, after the killing, by police, of Mark Duggan. The Occupy movement was born on the University of California campuses, and then reborn as a worldwide phenomenon, and by the time I needed to describe the effects of tear gas for a novel about the 1970s, all I had to do was walk downtown to Occupy's encampment, or watch live feeds from Oakland, California.

In 1978, the Red Brigades killed Aldo Moro, the leader of the Christian Democrats and former prime minister of Italy. That same year, Guy Debord, founder of the Situationist International, made his final film, *In girum imus nocte et consumimur igni*, its title a famous Latin palindrome, translatable as "we turn in the night and are consumed by fire." The film includes many still images that I looked at and into as I wrote. Debord's relationship to women and girls is so strange. He's suggesting they've been used for banal consumer culture—to sell soap, for instance—and yet surely he enjoys seeing them in their bikinis, their young flesh and sweet smiles, as he edits them into the frame.

As I was working on my novel, I encountered a woman who was friends with the only Situationist not expelled from the group by Debord, the enigmatic, semi-infamous Gianfranco Sanguinetti. "What is he up to?" I asked a little too eagerly. "What does he do now?" She shrugged and, coolly, disdainfully, said, "He lives." Later, I learned that Sanguinetti had a large inheritance, and that he mostly tended "his vineyards and his orchards." In addition, I learned that those who "live" can afford to.

A few more films besides Debord's that were important sources: Barbara Loden's *Wanda*, about a woman who isn't afraid to throw her life away. Chantal Akerman's *News from Home*, in which the camera wanders the deserted streets of Lower Manhattan. Alberto Grifi and Massimo Sarchielli's *Anna*, the mother of all films about Italy in the 1970s. Also, a filmic fact: that *Taxi Driver* was re-rated from X to R after Scorsese scaled back the brightness of reds in the film printing. Michel Auder's *The Feature*, which I saw at Anthology Film Archives, just me and one old man crinkling a paper bag in the theater, as Auder spent Cindy Sherman's money on prostitutes, playing himself in a despicable but brilliant game. Before he was married to Cindy Sherman, Auder had been with Viva, the Warhol superstar. Viva later dated the photographer William Eggleston, when she was living at the Chelsea Hotel, just after he made *Stranded in Canton*, in which his Memphis friends wave guns and hold forth in Quaalude slurs.

*   *   *

An appeal to images is a demand for love. We want something more than just their mute glory. We want them to give up a clue, a key, a way to cut open a space, cut into a register, locate a tone, without which the novelist is lost.

It was with images that I began *The Flamethrowers*. By the time I finished, I found myself with a large stash.

Jack Goldstein, *The Murder*, 1977, 33⅓ RPM.

This twelve-minute record is a montage of sound effects—mostly breaking glass, pouring rain, and thunder. The artist Jack Goldstein had all the right ingredients for myth: brilliant, cool, mysterious. He was hugely influential but ended up living in a trailer in East LA, selling ice cream from a truck. The ice cream once melted completely when he had to wait in line for methadone, but he refroze it and sold it anyway. He died in 2003, and so his body of work is now, sadly, a bounded set.

William Eggleston, still from *Stranded in Canton*, 1974.

There's a scene in *Stranded in Canton* in which Memphis local Jim Dickinson, who produced an album for the band Big Star, leers into the camera in rhinestone-rimmed glasses. He and an unnamed woman kiss, but they are high on Quaaludes and sort of miss each other's lips. He's wearing an ugly tuxedo, as if he's on his way to a high school prom. I have watched *Stranded in Canton* many times; it stays mysterious. There are two different dentists who each figure prominently, one shirtless, both drunk. Those dentists are dead now, as are many, if not most, of the people in the video. According to the credits, a not insignificant portion of them were murders or suicides. Neither tragic nor legendary, I myself will never die.

Larry Fink, *Black Mask*, 1967.

Black Mask was a Dada-inspired antiwar movement that intervened in culture and politics and later morphed into Up Against the Wall Motherfucker, "a street gang with an analysis." They ran soup kitchens and a free store and tried to empower and motivate the disenfranchised. Their legacy made way for the great culture of East Village artists' squats like the Gas Station on Avenue B.

Danny Lyon, *88 Gold Street*, 1967.

The same year Larry Fink photographed Black Mask on Wall Street, Danny Lyon methodically captured with a view camera the vast demolition of Lower Manhattan, much of it coming down for the construction of the Twin Towers. Factories and warehouses to be replaced by finance, which gives literal shape to a significant transformation of the seventies: the death of American manufacturing.

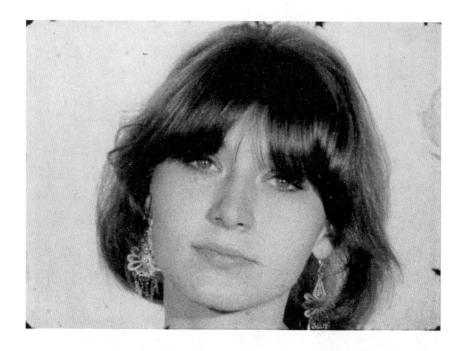

Andy Warhol, still from *Screen Test: Virginia Tusi*, 1965.

Who is she? No one seems to know. "A young woman identified only as Virginia Tusi," according to the catalogue raisonné. She was included in Warhol's *Thirteen Most Beautiful Women* along with Susanne De Maria and Julie Judd—the exceptionally pretty wives of Walter De Maria and Donald Judd. Warhol's two favorite kinds of people were beautiful people and the American upper classes. When those were combined into one person, such as Edie Sedgwick: bliss. One of the more striking men that Warhol filmed in 1965 was in the audience when I saw a program of *Screen Tests* in 2011. This man, a beard now tumbling down his chin, big belly protruding from his open blazer, shared anecdotes. "Warhol wanted me to flex my jaw," he said. And, "Edie was a real bitch." It might be better if Virginia Tusi just keeps beaming resplendently from her *Screen Test*, a mystery of mute loveliness.

Julie Buck and Karin Segal, *China Girl #56*, ca. 1970s, restored and transferred 2005.

China Girls, whose faces were used to adjust color densities in film processing, were mostly secretaries who worked in the film labs—regular women who appeared on leader that was distributed all over the world. It's not clear why they had that rather racist moniker; some say the original ones were Asian, and others speculate that a particular secretary who posed for film leader was a habitual server of tea (which makes the name seem even more problematic). China Girls were used indexically to calibrate skin tone, meaning *white* skin tone; racial bias is right there on the leader, in the form of a smiling secretary. In France, they were "*les lilis.*" If the projectionist loaded the film correctly, you didn't see the China Girl. And if you did see her, she flashed by so quickly she was only a blur. They were ubiquitous and yet invisible, a thing in the margin that was central to each film, these nameless women who, as legend has it, were traded among film technicians and projectionists like baseball cards.

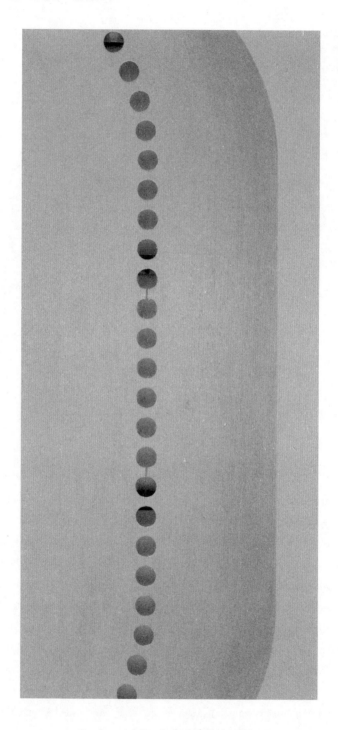

Lee Lozano, *Punch, Peek & Feel*, 1967.

Allen Ginsberg, *Sandro Chia*, 1985.

"In a serious confrontation, I'd take a shotgun, any day. It's a much more formidable and effective weapon than the handgun, unless it's a hand shotgun. I'd like to see more of those," wrote William Burroughs. The artist Sandro Chia had been firing at targets with Burroughs in Rhinebeck, New York, when this photograph by Allen Ginsberg was taken.

[Left] Lee Lozano was a tough and uncompromising person, celebrated by her male contemporaries for her conceptually driven paintings and the way she collapsed art into life. She had a solo show at the Whitney in 1970. In 1971, for her piece *Decide to Boycott Women*, she did just that: she didn't speak to women for the next twenty-eight years, right up until her death.

Robert Heinecken, *Cliché Vary: Autoeroticism*, 1974.

The sweet innocence of the McLuhan seventies. By the 1980s, when I was a teenager, I carried around a copy of *Subliminal Seduction: Are You Being Sexually Aroused by This Picture?* and thought I was being very ironic and clever. The culture by that point was already using the ability to decode to sell us to ourselves in even more effective ways. Selling us sex. Even as sex was, is, and will always be, one of the few things people can offer each other for free.

David Salle, *The Coffee Drinkers*, 1973.

She's having a quiet, contemplative moment in morning light. She's selling coffee. Or coffee's selling her, as her, or as . . . lifestyle? Something feminine, calming, pure? "Images that understand us" was a phrase coined by David Salle and James Welling. Salle, as a twenty-one-year-old student, made this prescient series—well before we came to know work by Richard Prince or Cindy Sherman—by photographing four women in his life (among them his girlfriend and mother) and gluing on the Nescafé label.

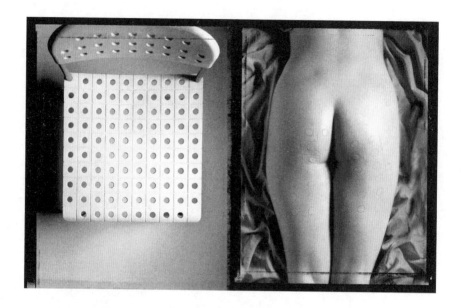

Gabriele Basilico, *Contact*, 1984.

"Putting together chairs and bottoms was very enjoyable for me," Gabriele Basilico said of his series *Contact*. He called the residual marks from this process "provisional relief tattoos." But tattoos of what? Modernism, as painless as modernism looks but never is. The link between violence and modernism is everywhere but too broad to get into in the form of a caption. It's something more like a life's work. Someone's, anyhow, if not mine.

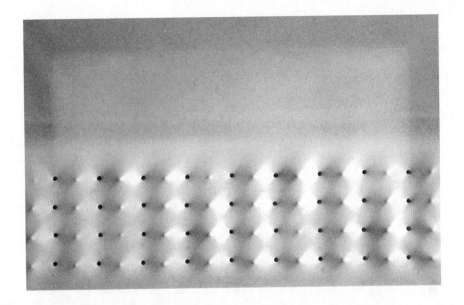

Enrico Castellani, *Superficie*, 2008.

Enrico Castellani, a younger contemporary of Lucio Fontana and Alberto Burri, was the first person in Italy targeted in the massive sweep of arrests in the seventies. Castellani seems to have circulated among leftists. A recent catalog of his work includes an essay by Adriano Sofri, former leader of the leftist group Lotta Continua, who spent twenty-two years in prison for instigating the assassination of a police captain (Sofri vehemently maintains his innocence).

Alberto Grifi and Massimo Sarchielli, still from *Anna*, 1975.

Later in this book, I write quite a bit about Anna, a homeless, pregnant, drug-addicted teen "adopted" by two male filmmakers in 1970s Rome. *The Flamethrowers* was in part dedicated to her, and to her disappearance as an act of revolt. An Austrian filmmaker, Constanze Ruhm, a kindred spirit in her interest in Anna, traveled to Sardinia, where Anna was from, to track her down. She'd apparently died in 2004. I would guess that Anna was less interested in the movie about her than I was, than Constanze was. The people I've known like Anna—and I've known many—they live in the present tense of their lives, not the past. Caught up, mired, and possessed by real time instead of nostalgia.

From the cover of *I Volsci* (March 1980), issue 10.

She doesn't look Italian, despite having appeared on the cover of an ultraleftist Roman newspaper. Some told me she was German, others that it was the photographer who was German. I'd reached deep into my connections to the older generation in Italy to try to find out who she was. No one could quite remember, from the hazy time of youth when you don't concern yourself with names and provenance. My publishers thought that the woman, discovering that her photo was on the cover of my book, might complain. Why would she do that? I asked. The response: "Let's say she changed her life and married a high-powered banker or well-known politician over there in Germany, and she hasn't told him about her radical past, but your book announces it." "But that would be a good story," I said, and they agreed. So far, no one has come forward claiming to have been this girl.

Tano D'Amico, *At the Gates of the University*, 1977.

Go to Italy and few mention the 1970s, when their country literally almost had a revolution. That explosive era and its joys, traumas, and failures have been all but erased. Luckily, there are some remainders, like the amazing photographs of Tano D'Amico. Here he captures the gates of Sapienza University in Rome on February 17, 1977, when it was occupied by students, as Luciano Lama, leader of the biggest labor union in Italy, came to pay them a visit and was heckled and expelled.

"Mara" is Mara Cagol, a former leader of Italy's leftist-militant Brigate Rosse (BR). "Le altre" are the militant women in Italy in the 1970s, whose Leninism and bombs were only one small and contested facet of a vast and complex wave of feminist actions that transformed the landscape of Italy. Ida Faré, coauthor of this book, was an important theorist of both feminism and architecture, a professor, activist, writer, and founding member of the Milan Women's Bookstore Collective. While writing *The Flamethrowers*, I was invited to the collective's monthly meeting and dinner. That night, Faré was the appointed host of our discussions. The other women in attendance that evening were all similarly legendary and radical figures of the 1970s. They wore black, chain-smoked, had perfectly coiffed hair, and they called each other gruffly by their last names. At dinner, they simultaneously scolded me for my ignorance and were incredibly generous and warm. Ida Faré died in 2018.

It's curious that for the cover of this book, an image from Godard's 1967 film *La Chinoise* was chosen. Not an image of a real female engaged in armed struggle, of which Italy produced several, but a still from a film where an actress (Juliet Berto) *plays* a terrorist, crouching behind a machine-gun turret built of stacked copies of Mao's *Little Red Book*. The real terrorist, Mara Cagol, successfully broke her husband, fellow BR leader Renato Curcio, from prison in 1975. The same year, she was gunned down in a shoot-out with carabinieri. The founder of Feltrinelli, the press that published this book, had died accidentally in 1972, attempting to sabotage Milan's power supply.

POPULAR MECHANICS

Ciro is the "good" brother in Luchino Visconti's 1960 film *Rocco and His Brothers*, the one who found a way to live in industrial Northern Italy: he accepts his social position as an unskilled worker on the assembly lines of Alfa Romeo, marries a nice local petty bourgeois girl, and lives cleanly. At the end of the film, Ciro has reported his brother Simone to the police. Rocco has gone off to pursue a career in the brutal world of professional boxing. The youngest brother, Luca, dreams of returning to the southern region of Lucania, where the brothers are from. But meanwhile, the family is shattered and dispersed.

Why would these people have left Lucania to begin with, a world where you relax in the sun, go to the beach, take a tomato from the vine when you're hungry? By 1960, there was chronic underemployment in the South. The soil was of poor quality. Grain markets had been deregulated, causing prices to plummet. For rural populations in the Mezzogiorno, there was no economic future.

At the same time, the Italian postwar economic "miracle" meant there were jobs in the factories of the rapidly industrializing North. Between 1951 and 1971, nine million people migrated from rural to industrial areas in Italy. They often arrived in the big cities with nothing, and were forced to live in train station waiting rooms or on relatives' floors. They worked shifts on building sites or in factories that offered long hours and treacherous conditions.

This history is all deftly evoked in *Rocco and His Brothers*, which ends after the Southerners hear the factory whistle and return from lunch to their shift on the assembly lines of Alfa Romeo. And yet the saga is not over; the end of the film opens outward to the portents of a tumultuous future. To what was to come, and eventually did come.

By 1969, the workers from the South on the assembly lines of the North revolted in waves of wildcat strikes and violence. This was a new movement, of workers that rejected the values of classic worker organizations, and most especially the Communist Party, which was regarded as a blockade to real change, an organ of compromise with company bosses. These workers were ready to reject the entire structure of Northern life and of work itself. Their revolt was an all-out assault on their own exploitation. They wanted "everything," as their placard slogan and shop-floor chant famously expressed, *Vogliamo tutto!*

We Want Everything, Nanni Balestrini's 1971 novel about this volatile historical moment, is a work of great energy and originality. It's also an unparalleled document of workerist history, and one that still resonates within the contradictions of the postindustrial present. Its artfulness emanates from tone: The person who speaks in this novel is nameless but intimate. He is insolent and blunt. He's full of personality, humor, and rage. He speaks in a kind of vernacular poetry that gets into the mind and stays there. "All this new stuff in the city had a price on it," he says, "from the newspaper to the meat to the shoes; everything had a price."

The protagonist has migrated from the South of Italy to Turin and is lucky enough to have a place to sleep at his sister's, while many of the "great tide" of Southerners washing into the city are living in the second-class waiting room at Porta Nuova train station, which would admit anyone with a Fiat ID card or a letter from Fiat stating that they had an interview at the factory. The police patrolled the train station vigilantly, but they weren't on the lookout for loiterers and squatters. The police were looking for journalists, making sure they didn't get anywhere near the second-class waiting room—"this dormitory, for free, that Fiat had at the Torino train station."

At the Fiat plant, our hero seeks employment along with twenty thousand other new hires. "The monsters were coming," he says, "the horrible workers," tolerated on account of the high demand for labor. The work is so unbearable that many new hires quit after just a few days. Some withstand only half a day before choosing destitution over the demands of the assembly line. The narrator is part of this tide of monsters, hated that much more because the factory needs them.

He goes through an interview process that is a pantomime (everyone is hired), then a company medical assessment, which is even more ridiculous. He endures muscle-strength testing on newfangled machinery, a blood test in a room that features high piles of stinking, blood-soaked cotton balls, and a piss test, for which the men are handed jars and "make beer" standing in a circle. During the subsequent doctor's examination, the narrator, seeing that the exam is a charade, announces that he is missing one testicle. He is hired despite this lie. "Maybe they wouldn't have taken a paraplegic," he speculates. But the medical exam has not been *entirely* a charade. It seems instead a necessary stage in these workers' exploitation: they are handing over the rights for the one thing they possess—their bodies—to the bosses of Fiat, transferring ownership of their selves to the factory. So when the narrator claims to the company doctor that he's only got one ball, he is throwing *them* an insult, telling them that their new acquisition is faulty; it's not even a complete man.

On the assembly line, the real fun begins. The work is backbreaking. In this era, wages were tied to productivity, meaning workers didn't get a decent base wage; they could not earn enough to live on unless they produced a certain profit margin for the company. At one point, the narrator is put on a line where the work requires use of just one shoulder to rivet with a heavy pneumatic gun, a repeated motion that will deform him by twisting his back and bulking his muscles asymmetrically. There are, meanwhile, some on the assembly line who are dedicated to work and to the Communist Party, Northerners from peasant backgrounds, "really hard people, a bit dense, lacking in imagination," people for whom "work was everything." To the narrator, they're worthless. "Only a drone," he says, "could spend years in this shitty prison and do a job that destroys your life."

The narrator gets sick leave but discovers that he has no idea how to deal with free time, how to relax or what to do in Turin. The factory not only degrades work; it degrades life away from work. This is alienation, the lived experience of exploitation, but it is demonstrated here without theoretical abstractions: it's an oral account of a person's days—that's all.

Eventually, the narrator decides to dedicate himself totally to making trouble. It's a commitment to risk everything. "I'm inside here just to make money and that's it," he tells his bosses at Fiat. "But if you piss me off and break my balls I'll smash your heads in, all of you." And so the struggle begins. But the narrator's threat, that scene, is not a moment of singular heroism. As literature and history both, *We Want Everything* is not a story of one remarkable man (history never is, even if novels so often rely on the myth of an avenging angel). The voice in the book could also be said to represent all the nameless and unknown who went North, like Rocco and his brothers, and like the twenty thousand who were hired alongside the novel's narrator in 1969. It's the story of the people who worked these awful jobs, blessed and burdened as they were with a masculine pride, a rage and strength and violence that they decided, all at once, to direct at factory bosses.

This struggle was about men; the women would not have their say quite yet. Women—exploited doubly in Italy, in the piecework they did at kitchen tables for the factories in the North, and by their families for their domestic labor—would have to mark out their own path, and did. In fact, feminism had the most lasting and successful impact among the demands made in the revolts of 1970s Italy. But women's demands were not part of the "everything" in this everything of factory revolts, a reminder that the word has limits, a context. "We want everything" meant we want to live lives with meaning, and we refuse to be forced to work in order to survive. It was a working-class-male "everything"; women would still be at home toiling away, even in the case of unlikely victory.

The second half of *We Want Everything* opens with a chapter on wages and marks the narrator's transformation into a theorist of his own struggle. He sees that, as a worker whose wages are tied to productivity, he collaborates with the bosses against himself. The tone makes a subtle shift. The "I" partly dissolves, and the book becomes something like pirate radio news bulletins of the war on the factory, the war in the streets. The struggle expands. The narrator, wherever he is now, is part of a new collective desire, calling not for higher base pay but for the abolition of capitalism, for the bosses' economy to collapse.

Before I'd learned much about the history of the factory struggles in Italy, I knew about Nanni Balestrini—which tells you that I didn't know very much about Balestrini. On a trip to Italy more than a decade ago, I decided to really take on learning about his work. I went to a Feltrinelli shop in Milan and bought a bunch of books. I brought them back to where I was staying, at the home of an old friend of mine, Claudio Guenzani, who is of the same generation as Nanni. "What do you think of this writer?" I asked. Claudio said, "What do I think of Nanni? When he was going to be arrested, I drove him to the Alps so he could escape Italy. He skied over to France, and I picked him up in Chamonix."

I had thought Claudio and I were going to discuss Nanni's poems, his art, his novels, possibly his politics—not a fugitive life. But life and politics and art are fused in the spirit of Balestrini. Hearing that Claudio helped him get to safety in France in the crackdowns of the late 1970s should have come as no surprise.

When Balestrini found out he was going to be arrested for "insurrectionary activities," Claudio had set him up with ski gear and skis and driven him to the Italian Alps. Claudio then drove into France and waited for him to ski down on the other side of Mont Blanc, into Chamonix. I pictured the one photo I'd seen of Balestrini, a man wearing a scarf wrapped in a complicated and elegant manner, a person who looked more bohemian and urbane than athletic. I asked, "But does Nanni *ski*?" Claudio held out his hands in equivocation and shrugged. "You know . . . good enough?" (I later learned that a ski instructor—Nanni's brother-in-law—had skied with him.)

Nanni Balestrini's novels have meant a great deal to me over the years. Formally, stylistically, they are in a category alone. Until I discovered them, I had often wondered if a novelist needed to have contempt for humanity, à la Céline, to have a great style. Style and cynicism—the ability to satirize, and to leave nothing sacred—had always seemed linked. In youth, I'd even regarded a lack of nihilism as an artistic weakness. Balestrini gives the lie to this idea. His novels, which are as funny and bleak as *Journey to the End of the Night*, are fueled not by contempt but instead by a kind of indestructible belief in revolutionary possibility. This may have something to do with the way the books were made. Balestrini was a subversive, an activist, and an organizer lifelong, in meetings, on barricades, outside factory gates, in the streets, in clandestine spaces. Never a voyeur, and always a participant, which must have been why people trusted him when he turned on his tape recorder. He was introducing art—the novel—to the work of rejecting, possibly overthrowing, bourgeois structures of power.

For *We Want Everything*, and also *The Unseen*—his novel about militants forced underground in the wake of the Autonomist actions of the 1970s—Balestrini recorded the voices of real people and then ventriloquized their stories in delirious and addictive run-on streams of "I," each voice a speck in the multitude, a witness. Not a person receding from the crowd, but the anonymous political subject, scored with the knife of history. What's singular about Balestrini's contribution to literature is not just his style but the way he upends the phantom qualifier "bourgeois" to the novel, a literary form traditionally predicated on consciousness as distance, distinction, observation, or inner experience. For *We Want Everything*, the voice came from that of a real person named Alfonso Natella. In converting the voice of Alfonso to a fictional narrator, Balestrini effectively created the voice incarnate of strike and riot—of sheer refusal as something like a spontaneous strategy.

Balestrini had been a founding member, in 1968, of the extra-parliamentary left-wing group Potere Operaio, whose focus was on factories and factory workers, on listening to workers and producing a movement of their voices and direct experience. It's likely that Balestrini was outside the gates of Fiat in 1969. This method of workers' inquiry, called "*inchiesta*" by its practitioners in Italy, has foundations in Marxism. The concept of collecting the stories of workers, the idea that their accounts of work and of their lives would be essential to any revolutionary process, goes all the way back to Marx's 1880 worker's questionnaire, which was meant to be disseminated among French factory workers. It is the "workers in town and country," Marx wrote, who "alone can describe with full knowledge the misfortunes from which they suffer." Simply put, there is no theory without struggle. Struggle is the condition of possibility for theory. And struggle is produced by workers themselves. But the practice of workers' inquiry didn't quite take hold in Europe until after World War II, in the tactics and tenets of the radical-left French group Socialism or Barbarism, which came to influence workerist theory—*Operaismo*—in Italy.

In its use by Balestrini, who was not just a militant and theorist but a poet and artist, a writer to the core, *inchiesta* became something more, something else: a singular artistic achievement and a new literary form, the novel-*inchiesta*. If the novel, traditionally, is a work of introspection, in Balestrini's hands it is instead a work of refraction: a way to refract that which "is already literature" even before its existence in a book, as Umberto Eco wrote of the voice in *We Want Everything*. One could argue that the passing thoughts of a worker on the assembly line are also already literature. And Balestrini skiing down the Mont Blanc, his scarf flapping—this is literature, too.

In making novels of the voices of people like Alfonso Natella—and also Sergio Bianchi, whose life story appears in *The Unseen*, and the narrator of *Sandokan*, who speaks of the impact of the Camorra on a small community in Southern Italy—Balestrini takes an outlook, the much-touted individual consciousness, and merges that consciousness with class, with social layers indivisible into lone lives. And yet the voices retain specificity—a set of attitudes, moods, prejudices, back-story—but they each speak in a way that exemplifies what life was like *for a person such as them*, in a moment when there were many like them. Balestrini's novels are works that capture and illuminate voice. Voices speaking, rather than words written. In this way, these works depart from the classical subjectivity of the nineteenth-century novel and seem closer to an earlier tradition, also oral and heroic and historic: epic poetry.

When he died in the spring of 2019, an hours-long celebration was held at Rome's Teatro Argentina to honor Balestrini, who hated funerals. The event was called "The greatest Nannis of our lives." Until that day, none of his very broad circle of friends and collaborators, a world of people involved in far-left politics of the 1970s, had ever met Alfonso Natella, the inspiration, allegedly, for the voice in *We Want Everything*. Some people even suspected there *was* no Alfonso—that he was an amalgamation of the many people Nanni would have met and organized alongside during the Hot Autumn of factory strikes in Milan and Turin, in 1969 and 1970. He turned out to be real. Almost fifty years after his appearance in *We Want Everything*, Alfonso walked into the Teatro Argentina and announced himself, finally showing his face in order to celebrate his departed friend.

After my novel *The Flamethrowers* was published, in which a character escapes Italy in the same way that Nanni did, on skis, Nanni himself got in touch with me, and we became friends. On a few occasions I tried asking him about his own flight over the Alps, but Nanni didn't really like questions. A question for him was often the path to banality.

Upon meeting him for the first time, I'd eagerly peppered him with questions about Alfonso Natella, and various people he'd known, about how he made his art, about the politics of Autonomia. He put his hand on my arm and said, "Look, let's talk about what wine to order. This is lunch. We are in a restaurant. Let's behave like normal people. We will decide what to eat, what to drink, even talk about the weather. The other stuff can wait."

At that lunch, in Rome in 2016, when we did eventually get to politics he was serious and astute, focused on life now and life in the future: not nostalgic, even as he wasn't hesitant to discuss the past. As he later told me, when I interviewed him more formally,

> More than being nostalgic, I consider myself lucky to have been through an extraordinary and happy period. But it would be senseless to search in that period for something anticipatory or something that could be applied politically in a radically different situation like the one we're living in forty years later. Everything is different, everything has changed. We need new ideas— and those are always more difficult to come up with. That period bequeaths us only a stimulus or, better, an imperative: that we need to change the world, and that this is possible, necessary, and urgent.

Nanni was a dandy and a gentleman; he'd greeted me at the airport the morning of our lunch in a pristine blazer and driving moccasins and escorted me by taxi into Rome. At the end of our day together, he walked me to Termini train station. We said goodbye at the point where only ticketed passengers are allowed through. I kept turning back, and Nanni remained standing where we had parted. He watched until my train arrived and I'd boarded. In that long, stretched interval, of watching him stand there waiting to see me depart, I knew I would never see him again, and I didn't, though we corresponded somewhat regularly.

Nanni never answered my central question about *We Want Everything*, regarding the life of Alfonso. Now, looking back, I'm not sure why this was so important to me. I think I could not fathom how it was that Nanni constructed a voice that sings with such particularity, comedy, force, and rage, and yet gives us a sense of thousands. Nanni was quite stubborn in his refusal to tell me anything about Alfonso. He said, "You're trying to force me to give Alfonso back his individuality. This is the opposite of what I wanted to do in the book, where he has no name. I can't do that."

For Nanni, an artistic imperative was an absolute imperative, and one that had consequences: to give Alfonso back his individuality would be to take away that very same individuality from all the nameless people to whom it came to belong—people who constituted a genuine social and political power, who lived both in the world and in the pages of Nanni's books.

THE SINKING OF THE HMS BOUNTY

This is what happened: my friend and I took a packed night train north from Florence, over the Alps to Munich. There were people sleeping on the luggage racks and in the aisles. My friend and I were crowded into the vestibule with at least twenty others. We rode standing, mashed shoulder to shoulder with strangers. I was against the door, on the metal scuff plate, which flips up when the door opens. If the train car door opened, there would be no place for me to stand.

Throughout the journey, I worked together with the other passengers at each railway stop. We pulled on the car door handle, against those on the platform, to prevent them from opening the door and getting on the train. There was snow in the mountains, though it was early October. We held the door against desperate and angry people banging on the windows and shouting, people no different from us— except that they were outside the train, not in, and there was no room for them.

We rode the night that way, drinking shared rotgut, swaying as one group of bodies, no room to sit. The Munich station into which we tumbled at dawn was cold and chaotic. A giant man came toward my friend and me with a big unwholesome grin. I remember his leather flight jacket, which squeaked as if it was new. He negotiated with my friend, who spoke German, and then we were slumped against the back seat of the man's Mercedes. He drove us what felt like a long ways, into a large park with various roadways, and in the park was a huge futuristic glass structure: the Olympic Stadium.

We followed the man into a set of apartments near the glass structure, down a hall and into a locker room to which the man had a set of keys. The locker room had cots in it, lined up. We gave the man money in exchange for this lodging and put our things into the lockers and then the man drove us to Oktoberfest, our destination, where people drank beer, ate roast chickens, fought, sang, threw their gnawed chicken bones into the corners of the beer hall, and lined up to take very long pisses.

When we were finished with all that, we set out for "home," a locker room of the 1972 Munich Olympics stadium. It was not easy to get there. We finally found the Olympic Park, where we stumbled and wandered. The park felt huge. It had no streetlights, or they were not on. The more we walked, the bigger and darker the place became, the longer this night. We skirted a large body of water. We thought we would never find the stadium, our overpriced cots in the locker room. We found instead a set of apartments and tried to break in, but without success. My friend climbed up a concrete wall that led to a second-floor balcony and tried the doors and windows of that unit, but it was also locked. Here my memory blurs. Did we get into these apartments? Or give up and eventually find our cots in the locker room? All I remember is the next morning, standing under water that was not sufficiently hot, in a chilly tiled room with a row of showers built for athletes, of which I was not one, and instead training only for another day of drinking beer and lining up to piss.

I was eighteen, about to turn nineteen, as I watched my friend scale the concrete wall and try to force open a door or window of those apartments. I knew nothing, not one thing, about what happened at the 1972 Olympics in Munich, but these were the infamous apartments where Israeli athletes were abducted before some were tortured and all were murdered. Stunned by my own youthful ignorance, I recently did a little research and came upon an image of rows of cots and thought I was looking at an image of the locker room of cots that the German man in the squeaking leather jacket had rented to us. Those are the cots! I thought, amazed. I had googled "Munich Olympics 1972." This was on my phone. Looking closer, I understood that the cots in the photograph, what I thought were cots, were actually coffins, each covered with a cloth. The German man with the keys would have rented those out too; he wasn't sentimental, so maybe I'm making too much of this.

When I heard the HMS Bounty had been destroyed, in 2012, I thought my favorite lounge and restaurant in Koreatown was gone. It's on the ground floor of the Gaylord, a residential hotel with an old-fashioned lobby and an equally old-fashioned lobby clerk.

"No," someone said, "the real HMS *Bounty*. The ship—it sunk. The crew had to be rescued by the coast guard. Two crew members drowned."

But wasn't the *Bounty* burned by mutineers some two hundred years ago? I'd asked.

The replica they made for the 1962 movie *Mutiny on the Bounty*, that was what sunk, it was explained to me.

The HMS Bounty that I knew, on Wilshire Boulevard, with its cozy booths, fish and chips, jukebox: Was it named after the model or the original? Which is the real HMS *Bounty*? If asked, although I have not been asked, I'd know the answer: the bar and restaurant, of course, on the ground floor of the Gaylord. I've been a patron there for twenty years. It has not sunk, but they took the omelet off the menu a few years back, just around the time my favorite waitress died of old age.

The HMS Bounty is across the street from where the Ambassador Hotel stood. Robert Kennedy was assassinated there. It was demolished in 2006. In the years before (it had closed as a hotel in 1989), you could go inside only if you were part of a film or TV crew staging a production on its grounds. People used the backdrop of the Ambassador, which had been gorgeously renovated in 1949 by pioneering black architect Paul Revere Williams, to represent all manner of lavish surroundings, but never to represent the Ambassador Hotel itself. If you were part of a team disguising the hotel as a fictional setting, and you were willing to pay, they would let you in to wander the place.

> "Salt water on the tennis courts can be quite a nuisance . . ."

> "All our love, scribbled down
> On a cardboard box before drowning . . ."

> "We are still alive, one of us said."

Those are lines I've pulled from "The Sinking of the *Titanic*" by the renowned German poet Hans Magnus Enzensberger.

> "Sometimes I don't know 'myself.' I am second-rate.
> My hand trembles. It is not the gin.

It is not fame. It is history
with its unending sham and duplicity."

"True, the reproduction of a lifeboat
does not save anybody, the difference
between a life jacket and the term *life jacket*
makes the difference between survival and death—

But the dinner is going on regardless . . ."

Hans Magnus Enzensberger is a chain-smoking dandy who wears seersucker in the summertime. His eyes are blue crystals that emit rays of light and seem to put him at godlike counterpoise to the sentimental and false. I met him a few years ago, in Denmark. He outdrank and outlived me every moment I was near him. At the time, he was eighty-five. A group of us toured the house of the writer Karen Blixen, now a museum, which was adjacent to our hotel. Some knew her as Isak Dinesen. Her friends called her "Tania." But only Carson McCullers decided to address her as "Mac," when they lunched together on champagne and oysters.

One night I said something banal to Hans Magnus that I didn't really myself believe, about admiring the Danish design in the lobby of our hotel, relentless Scandinavian design, which neither of us had found any way to escape that whole week in Denmark. I pretended I liked all this blocky furniture and the square-shouldered women's clothes, the Lucite umbrella stands. I praised the design for no reason except that its omnipresence had seduced me into thinking these weird objects in every room were superior to normal life. As I spoke to Hans Magnus, the only thing in my sight line that wasn't a gleaming Lucite cube or ceramic cube or a white leather cube was Hans Magnus's dirty cigarette. He looked at me and said, about the Danish design, "But would you want to *live* with it?" His cigarette smoke curled. That curl was the promise of the other world, lived without it: a bare room in Germany, soot coming down in flakes. He's right. I want the bare room, the blank starting point for seeing.

Smoke from a cigarette is often called blue. We know just what they mean when they say the smoke is blue. It's literal—it *is* bluish—but a specific blue that is the compression of reality into sign.

Photography is cataloged as mimesis, unlike painting or sculpture, which produces only likeness or abstraction. The art historian Rosalind Krauss wrote famously that the achievement of surrealist photography was in the paradox of capturing a faithful trace of a reality that is *already constituted as a sign*, so that the reality-trace of the photograph reveals a real that is actually a symbol, or wavers between symbol and real, such as in Man Ray's famous *Ingres's Violin*, a photograph of a woman's back with two f-holes overlaid, connecting the shape of her body ("reality") to the shape of the instrument ("sign"), and convulsing the image.

But what about the paradox of reality constituted as sign—a photograph—of a *sign* constituted as *reality*? That's the tension in an image by the German artist Thomas Demand, who reconstructs photographed scenes out of paper, for instance a violin workshop, or the exterior of a modest house with a view behind it of blooming cherry trees, and then he photographs this reconstructed, paper simulacrum. The special connection to reality, "with which all photography is endowed," according to Rosalind Krauss, does not quite apply. It does and does not apply. Krauss likens photography to fingerprints. To the rings that cold glasses leave on tables. A photograph, she writes, is closer to a death mask or the tracks of a gull on a beach than it is to a painting or sculpture. It's the residue of things we see, rather than a reconstruction of things we see. But the photographs that Thomas Demand takes of the photographed scenes he reconstitutes from paper do not present a straight trace of reality, the glass ring on the table, the track of the gull on the beach. They offer, instead, a trace of a model of a trace of reality.

Another German artist, Hanne Darboven, inscribed human time—via music—onto the picture plane, onto paper. "Timeswings," she called these marks. They are human breaths, the life she spent working. Darboven worked eighteen hours a day, slept little, smoked constantly. It's all there in those timeswings. Thomas Demand uses paper to make images that exclude time. He tombifies reality. It is not made dead but made impossible. The images are vacuums. They do not suffocate us, since we are only looking. But much can be felt through the eyes. I don't know about you, but a whiff of suffocation is enough suffocation for me.

Tallulah Bankhead is the first one into the lifeboat in the 1944 Alfred Hitchcock movie *Lifeboat*, after a German U-boat blows up a merchant marine vessel on which she was a passenger. Rescued, she is the foundational conditions of the lifeboat and movie: woman, fur coat, brandy, typewriter, diamond bracelet, sarcasm, wit. She is the tennis court with salt water on it. Things float past: flotsam. People climb on, the other few survivors, and coalesce into a movie cast. A stranger, the last one pulled on board, is the great conceit of the film. "*Danke schön,*" he says to the rest. He turns out to be the captain of the U-boat that blew up the ship all these survivors were on.

There is a palazzo on the Grand Canal in Venice that I remember as a melting ship, a melting clock, one side sinking, the other shored up and restored. It's called the Palazzo Contarini degli Scrigni. The Contarini family owned it. *Scrigno* means "casket," which is a container for bodies or gold. The Contarini family employed Palladio. I cut my hands making my Palladio Rotonda from foam core as an undergrad. I was a student passingly interested in architecture on account of a charismatic teacher named Lars Lerup. My rotunda was empty of people and ideas. It was a copy, and a copy can make a volume that might be filled with ideas but mine, as I said, stayed empty.

In Alexander Kluge's film about Hans Magnus Enzensberger's "The Sinking of the *Titanic*," an image flashes by, a still that is a colored illustration of people in a movie theater. On the screen is a sinking ship, peril in progress. A woman in the back of the theater is standing, her arms thrown high in fear and anguish for those who are drowning. She is watching a movie of a sinking ship. It is a fiction, but her terror is real. Except her terror can't be real, since she is drawn. She's just a drawing.

I am not quite afraid of the act of dying, of transition. There is a motor lodge called the Portal Motel and I thought it was in Lucerne, but it's in Lone Pine, the town of Lone Pine, unless there are two. Two portals. The Portal Motel seems like a good place to go. I am not afraid of dying, like I said. What I fear is to be dead. I dread the end. Not coming, but arrived.

In the work of Thomas Demand, "Do not disturb" is not a phrase but a shape—a vertical rectangle with a hole at the top for a doorknob. Also, it's a relation: a tag that sits on a doorknob or latch. It can be any color and still be recognized, even red, which is what he makes it. In a ship novel I'm fond of, couples licit and illicit are always sneaking off to staterooms. The novel's narrator walks past a door wedged open. He sees a girl in postcoital glow ironing the white uniform pants of the ship's wireless operator. The wireless operator lounges on the bed, nude. Do Not Disturb.

Thomas Demand re-created the exterior of the Cambridge apartment where Tamerlan Tsarnaev lived, its drab vinyl siding and, beyond a fence, a peek of blooming cherry trees. It's an exterior that is typical and drab. It's a house of no distinction. One could say this house would not "exist," certainly not as a photographed place, were it not for the fact that the person who lived there bombed the Boston Marathon. When power and history each shines its light, to say, *This ordinary and glum house is where a terrorist lived*, a source is born, an image that is created in the wake of destruction, a properly Hegelian birth. As an ordinary and glum apartment house, it's just one among millions of others.

The blossoms of cherry trees, like the ones that fill the background of the image of Tamerlan Tsarnaev's house, are the manifestation of an eternal return, but a simple one: spring. I'd rather live among trees than in the part of the mind that contemplates eternity. Seasons take place in time. Eternity means "outside of time" rather than endless. We do not know that cherry blossoms will eternally bloom. Each time they bloom gives joy that feels like a miracle. Feels, in other words, like a singular event.

Snow, another cyclical wonder, is the world's attempt at self-burial. Then it melts.

> I really don't like it when I have one ear pressed against
> the pillow and I start to hear my heart beat, who can
> sleep with all that noise

Dzhokhar Tsarnaev tweeted this before he followed his older brother, Tamerlan, over a cliff. Got a death sentence. Apologized, privately, to a Roman Catholic nun.

A few years ago I was in Eufaula, Alabama, for a family reunion, not my own but my in-laws'. I stopped at a thrift store. Walking the aisles, I came upon a dollhouse with a yellow plastic roof. I know that roof, I told myself. I know that house. The blue tulip silhouettes on the window shutters. I knew everything. I peered in the little windows at the little kitchen and the tiny bathroom and the photograph of wood grain papering the "den." (Did anyone ever have a den, or just fictional people on television shows, and the implied fictional people whom doll-houses bespeak?) This dollhouse was stained and dirty—it had a layer that marked it as not mine—but its rooms were primal scenes to which I held claims, to which I was returning, inside this thrift store in Eufaula, Alabama. I had owned this model of dollhouse—a menagerie, as I under-stood, peering in the windows, of everything that grips me and won't let go.

Since the little house already owned me, there was no need to buy it.

It is amazing what, from the past, you can drag into your net, only to find that it has never left your net.

At a restaurant in Venice the old waitress insisted we not order, and instead, she commanded that we be served "the catch of the day." The catch of the day were these burglar-mugged fishies, bottom-feeders that looked like cartoon drawings of bank robbers, proletarian faces, deep-fried. As a bourgeois, my decency was offended. Or maybe I was offended that these little scofflaws got caught in a dragnet, and I felt for them. Anyhow the waitress forgot to bring silverware.

It's said that capitalism relies on a system of selling something you don't own to someone who doesn't want it. Which is identical to how a Lacanian defines love. The lover makes a gift of his banality as if it were a wonder. He pretends to offer something more than his banality, a piece of the world that reflects his love and that he does not, in reality, possess. In both cases, love and futures, you force something you don't own onto someone who does not want it.

Capital requires the confidence that you can do business with time. Alain Badiou says the revolution to come seems impossible only if you swallow the lie that the present is viable and coherent. Once you see how impossible life already is, then the chance for a real, true, actual emancipatory horizon comes into view. Got it?

Many want to speculate on the future, the after-capitalism, but first we must define what capitalism is. If we don't define it, we cannot know its properties, or declare its death or its triumph, or even identify its health, ailing or robust. You have to understand capitalism perfectly to know if the universe of free markets is shaped like a cake donut— a three-torus topology—or is, in fact, a limitless reality, as it wants us to believe. Just to be clear, I don't count myself among those who do understand it, not even imperfectly.

The robotic arms on an auto assembly line work together so smoothly, they are almost intimate. They can achieve maximum closeness, one machine part to another, without any touching. They are not like humans. A shop floor of robots needs no bathroom booze, no love in a closet, no fistfights with labor bosses. Each time the machines pause their perfect movements, we see a still life. They become fixed, inanimate, in their tiny pauses. We know a little about those who suffered, lost jobs, when the robots came. Those who lost jobs do not lurk at the factory gates. They went into the service industry. The service industry is not actually "an industry." It is everything that is not manufacturing or agriculture. It is a not-thing.

I'm not the first to assert that reality itself has become false, an ideology, a fiction, a novel. Many understand this, that reality is an argument for itself and not a real, true thing.

God was ejected when we traveled from the closed world to the infinite universe. We were also ejected. Everyone was suddenly homeless, no longer happy in those ages when the starry sky was "the map of all possible paths," as Georg Lukács half-laments. The stars remained the same, except moving and not fixed, no longer part of our world, no longer part of us. Marguerite Duras says either God rules over a void—a universe in which we are the sole accident—or He only rules over us, which makes Him merely a "regional" God. A local. A townie.

What is objective and definite? Or rather, what is the sound of what is objective and definite? Feminine screams, and the breaking of glass.

In the Doge's Palace in Venice there is a room that was once the largest indoor gathering place in all of Europe. Capacity was two thousand important men. The doges ruled Venice for one thousand years. There were 120 of them. The term of service was life. Around the upper edges of this grand salon are painted portraits of the first seventy-six doges. All, that is, but one, a single Venetian doge who is represented by no portrait and instead a black banner, and on the black banner, text in Latin that reads: Here is the space reserved for Marino Faliero, decapitated for crimes.

Marino Faliero was doge for only one year. One year of one thousand. One doge of 120. And yet: anyone who has ever been in the grand council chamber of Venice, once the largest indoor gathering space in all of Europe, in fact anyone at all asked to name a Venetian doge, a single one, any doge of Venice, will name Marino Faliero. Or, if they don't recall his actual name, when asked if they can name a Venetian doge, people will answer, "The one whose memory they tried to erase. That's the one I know."

DURAS WITH AN S

If the French writer Marguerite Duras was an acute analyst of sorts (Jacques Lacan declared her the unwitting embodiment of his theories), she was also a one-woman Shock Doctrine, moving into sites of catastrophe not for the sake of extracting profit but in order to build narratives from her trademark materials of passion, grief, and silence.

In the opening montage of the movie *Hiroshima mon amour*, whose script she penned, the film camera glides through Hiroshima's Peace Memorial Museum, pausing before various reconstructions of horror—masses of anonymous hair, a gnarled, heat-blasted bicycle, a photograph of the bombed city reminiscent of *Guernica*—before moving on to a pearl-encrusted gift-shop model of the Palace of Industry, a symbol of the city's once-thriving military-industrial production, and then to a bus with the words "Atomic Tours" printed on its side. An attractive young tour guide speaks cheerfully through a microphone to passengers as the bus motors through "New" Hiroshima, which is spare, modern, angular, clean. The subtext of director Alain Resnais's montage is barely sub: industrial capitalism, urban culture, and eternal war are not just interrelated but on some level indistinguishable.

True enough, but not quite the desublimation that Duras was after. Over Resnais's montage, we hear the voice of an unnamed French woman, played by Emmanuelle Riva, claiming to have "seen everything" of the catastrophe at Hiroshima. An unnamed Japanese man, played by Eiji Okada, rebukes her claim ("you've seen nothing"). The French woman and Japanese man have met in Hiroshima, the site of an erased catastrophe where they carry on a brief and intense love affair.

As the narrative unfolds, it becomes clear that the woman's claim of having witnessed the nuclear holocaust is a fantasy along the lines of a screen memory—in strictly Freudian terms, a false or insignificant memory that defensively masks a real and traumatic one, in this case the fatal shooting of her German lover at the liberation of occupied Nevers, an episode she speaks of for the first time to the Japanese man, a cultural Other who enables her to revisit the original traumatic event. We shift, indirectly, from those masses of anonymous hair to the image of the woman's shaved head; from the atomic-baked bicycle to her own bike ride into Paris, as she emerges from a state of emotional death, madness, baldness. She is finally well enough to venture out. Her hair has grown. The night is warm. The war has officially ended, a denouement brought on by the dropping of atomic bombs. She joins the delirious crowd pouring into the streets.

Mysteriously, Marguerite Duras gave her friend Georges Bataille her share of windfall profits from *Hiroshima mon amour*. It isn't clear why. In 1957, she'd interviewed Bataille on the subject of "sovereignty," a theme he'd addressed in a 1949 essay on Hiroshima, in which he wrote that the instant of the nuclear blast was the only sovereign truth Hiroshima offered us. He'd gone on to declare that instant, that blast, "a vanishing splendor." Duras was herself not such a sick puppy as Bataille, but the common interpretation of her script for *Hiroshima mon amour* as "anti-nuclear," a treatise on peace, is not quite correct. It's more accurate to say that Duras both condemned human suffering and then again framed it as the only vital condition for the possibility of meaning.

A lot happened to Marguerite Duras. She lost a child while giving birth, and in that experience lost God and gained unwanted knowledge of death. Her husband Robert Antelme was deported to Dachau, came back, but weighing eighty pounds. Duras worked for the Occupation, and later joined the Resistance, then the Communist Party. Was expelled from the Communist Party but remained a Marxist. Duras had public dialogues with President François Mitterrand and Jean-Luc Godard, and for several years she hosted episodes of the French television show *Dim Dam Dom*, on which she interviewed a prostitute, a female prison warden, and a seven-year-old boy. Aspects of her life are legends, like the destitute poverty of her childhood in Indochina. In some writings, her mother's ailment is madness. In others, menopause. Or financial ruin. Sometimes, the mother's madness is her strength. Maybe these are not contradictions.

Things happened to Duras "that she never experienced," as she put it. The story of her life did not exist, she said. The novel of her life—yes. She obsessively read Proust, Conrad, and Ecclesiastes. She pursued a poetic absorption in the sacred and secret. She may have engendered a trend called autofiction, but she dismissed trends, and more important, she was adamant that the genre of autobiography was base, degraded. Same with "essayistic" writing. She resisted the anti-novel rhetoric of the practitioners of the Nouveau Roman, whom she called "businessmen." Literature was her interest, *that* kind of truth.

Marguerite wasn't always Duras. She was born Donnadieu, but with the publication of her first novel, *Les impudents*, in 1943, she went from Donnadieu to Duras and stayed that way. She chose as her alias the village of her father's origins, distancing herself from her family and binding her to the emanations of that place-name, which is pronounced with a regionally southern preference for a sibilant *s*. The village of Duras is in Lot-et-Garonne, an area south of the Dordogne and just north of Gascony. The language of Gascon, from which this practice of a spoken *s* derives, is not considered chic. Educated French people not from the region might be tempted to opt for a silent *s* with a proper name. In English, one hears a lot of Dur*aah*—especially from people who consider themselves Francophiles. Duras herself said Dur*aas*, and that's the correct, if unrefined, way to say it. With an *s*.

Proust, whom Duras admired a great deal, modeled the compelling and ridiculous Baron de Charlus on Robert de Montesquiou, of Gascony. Some argue that on account of Montesquiou's origins, Charlus should be pronounced Charl*uss*. In *Sodom and Gomorrah*, Proust himself makes quite a bit of fun of the issue of pronunciations and how they signify class and tact, and specifically the matter of an *s*, of guessing if it's silent or sibilant. Mme de Cambremer-Legrandin experiences a sort of rapture the first time she hears a proper name *without* the sibilant *s*—Uz*ai* instead of Uz*ès*—and suddenly the silent *s*, "a suppression that had stupefied her the day before, but which it now seemed so vulgar not to know," becomes the proof, and apotheosis, of a lifetime of good breeding and "smartness."

So vulgar not to know, and yet what Proust is really saying is that it's equally vulgar to be so conscious of elite significations, even as he, too, was entranced by the world of them. Mme de Cambremer-Legrandin is, after all, a mere bourgeois who elevated her station through marriage, and her self-conscious, snobbish, silent *s* will never change that, and can only ever be a kind of striving, made touchingly comical in *Sodom and Gomorrah*. Duras is something else. No tricks, full *s*. Maybe, in part, her late-life and notorious habit of referring to herself in the third person was a reminder to say it the humble way,

Dur*aas*. Or maybe it was just an element of what some labeled her narcissism, which seems like a superficial way to reject a genius. Duras was consumed with herself, true enough, but almost as if under a spell. Certain people experience their own lives very strongly. Regardless, there is a consistent quality, a kind of earthy simplicity, in all of her novels, films, plays, screenplays, and notebooks, and in the dreamily precise oral "telling" of *La Vie matérielle*, which is a master index of Durassianisms, of *s*-ness: lines that function on boldness and ease, which is to say, without airs.

> "There is one thing I'm good at, and that's looking at the sea."
> "When a woman drinks it's as if an animal were drinking, or a child."
> "Alcohol is a substitute for pleasure though it doesn't replace it."
> "A man and a woman, say what you like, they're different."
> "A life is no small matter."

Her assertions have the base facticity of soil and stones, even if one doesn't always agree with them, especially not with her homophobia, which gets expressed in the section of *La Vie matérielle* on men and seems to have gotten worse as her life fused into a fraught and complicated autumn-spring intimacy with Yann Andréa Steiner, who was gay.

La Vie matérielle was translated as *Practicalities* by Barbara Bray, but might be more felicitously titled "material life" or "everyday life." The book began as recordings of Duras speaking to her son's friend Jérôme Beaujour. After the recordings were transcribed, there was much reworking and cutting and reformulating by Duras. In terms of categories, the book is unique, but all of Duras's writing is novelistic in its breadth and profundity, and all of it can be poured from one flask to another, from play to novel to film, without altering its Durasness. In part, this is because speech and writing are in some sense the same thing with Duras. When she talks, she is writing, and when writing, speaking. (Some of her later work was spoken first to Yann Andréa, who typed her sentences, and the results were novels, such as *The Malady of Death*.) The English-edition flap copy describes *La Vie matérielle* as "about being an alcoholic, about being a woman, and about being a writer." And it is about those things—and more or less in that order—although drinking is woven throughout. Her discussions of it are blunt. They are also accurate, spoken by one who knows. When Duras made this book, in 1987, she had suffered late-stage cirrhosis, quit, started again, and lost her mind in a detox clinic, an episode she refers to, in the book, as a "coma." In 1988, her drinking put her in a real coma, for five months. "It's always too late when people tell someone they drink too much," she writes. "You never know yourself that you're an alcoholic. In one hundred percent of cases, it's taken as an insult."

Her talk of women and domestic life is of her era, although she was her own sort of early feminist, who felt that pregnancy was proof of superiority over men, which she constantly reminded the men around her while pregnant with her son Jean. In a section called "House and Home" she provides a list of important items with which she stocked Neauphle-le-Château, the country place where she wrote and where many of her films were made. The list includes butter, coffee filters, steel wool, fuses, and Scotch-Brite. Only frivolous women, she says, neglect repairs. For the "rough" work that men do, in counterpart to domestic chores, she is unimpressed: "To cut down trees after a day at the office isn't work, it's a kind of game." And even worse, she adds, a man thinks he's a hero if he goes out and buys a couple of potatoes. "Still, never mind," she finishes off, and in the next paragraph announces that people tell her she exaggerates, but that women could use a bit of idealizing. From there she is on to the burning of manuscripts, which makes the house feel virginal and clean, and her next topic, rolled into seamlessly, is the phenomenon of "sales, supersales, and final reductions" that drive a woman to purchase clothing she does not want or need. A woman ends up with a sartorial excess that is new to her generation, and yet this ur-woman, a figment of typicality, maintains the same role, in the home and in the world, that has persisted for all women in all times: a "theatre of profound loneliness that has constituted their lives for centuries."

At the end of *La Vie matérielle*, she is home from the hospital after a detoxification cure. She sees things that are "brighter than reality, as if lit from within." A woman in her bathroom holds a dead child. Every night Duras is "attacked by the 'people' lurking in the apartment." She describes an encounter with a "terrifying" man, a hallucination, as if this man is perfectly real, and he is: he is part of her fictive universe, the primal scenes she spent her life rendering and reworking, telling, and telling again.

Much of her publishing career was an encounter with misogyny: in the 1950s, male critics called her talent "masculine," "hardball," and "virile"—and they meant these descriptors as insults! (This kind of confused insistence on gendered literary territories has still not gone away, sadly.) The implication was that as a meek and feeble female, she had no right to her aloof candor, her outrageous confidence. And it's true that you'd have to think quite highly of your own ideas to express them with such austerity and melodrama, but that is the great paradox, and tension, of the equally rudimentary and audacious style of Duras. "People who say they don't like their own books, if such people exist, do so because they haven't learned to resist the attraction to humiliation," she wrote in one of her journals. "I love my books. They interest me."

Jean-Marie Straub and Danièle Huillet, who adapted a short story by Duras into a film called *En rachâchant*, said of their own work that it was best understood by cavemen and children. In fact, their work is difficult to understand by anyone not versed in literature, philosophy, and art, and moreover anyone not trained to watch difficult films, but their intentions in making such a claim seem clear enough: if you don't get it, you're judging it through an adapted set of ideologies and traditions that are obstacles, and once you unlearn your bad training, you will understand our movies. Their caveman is a kind of negative, the inverse shadow of cultural bias, an innocent. Fittingly, the Duras story they adapted is about a boy who learns without being taught, who knows things without the corruption of intellect.

Unlike Straub and Huillet, Duras might actually have a decent chance with cave people and children. Receiving the full impact of her work has little to do with education, erudition. You either relate to it or you don't. She could talk to anyone, and replicate any kind of voice (while somehow maintaining that tone, her *s*), like those of the curt but philosophical concierge and street sweeper who both feature in *Madame Dodin*. The moments of truth in her work are elemental and felt, not synthetic or abstruse. She told the actress Delphine Seyrig she might give up writing and open a service station for trucks along the highway.

Meanwhile, she was much loved and admired by many twentieth-century intellectuals, such as Lacan and Maurice Blanchot, both of whom wrote about her work ("I never understood much of him," she said of Lacan). Samuel Beckett credited hearing her radio play of *The Square* as a significant moment in his own creative life. She had what both Beckett and the filmmaker Alain Resnais admired as "tone." Durassian. Everything she made was marked by it, and the distinct quality of that tone is certainly what led to the accusation, fair enough, that she was at risk sometimes, if inadvertently, of self-caricature. But every writer aspires to have some margin of original power, a patterning and order that comes to them as a gift bestowed and is sent to no one else. If Duras wasn't so lucky, if she wasn't such a natural writer, her critics would have no object for their envy, their policing of excess, as well as the inverse—a suspicion of her restrained economy with words.

Her early writings, from her notebooks, evince her gift for fiction. None of it reads like a diary, even when the experiences are ones we know are close to her biography. Much of it is in third person, as if she were already controlling the levers of character, and the entries include crafted dialogue, artful gaps, compression. "At one time," she writes of childhood, "we used to feast on the pickled flesh of young crocodiles, but in the end we tired of everything." In an early draft of *The Sea Wall*, the sea, "making itself at home, would come in and scorch the crops." In an unpublished story called *Theodora*, a knack for insinuating authorial intrusion, metafictional, but not distancing, is already present: "Her eyes are green and shining, her dress is red, that's the situation." In the early drafts from the notebooks of *The War*, she powerfully conveys the chaos of waiting to learn of her husband's fate in a concentration camp. "I know everything you can know," she writes, "when you know nothing." A woman waits to get news of her daughter, chattering that she's had new taps put on her daughter's shoes, but then blurts that her daughter has probably been gassed. "With her stiff leg," the mother says, "they'll have gassed her."

In a section about losing her own baby in childbirth, a nurse says to her, "When they're that little, we burn them." The piece ends, "People who believe in God have become complete strangers to me." The notebooks are full of that tone, that s: high stakes and brute experience.

By the time she wrote *The Lover*, Duras was seventy years old. The book, some may forget, begins with a man telling her he prefers her face "as it is now. Ravaged." But she remained, according to men I've spoken to who knew her, devastatingly sexy, even in her advanced age. My surprised reaction makes one of these men, the film director Barbet Schroeder, laugh. It suggests a hopeless ignorance of the force of Duras. Does it matter that she was sexy? In a sense, yes, because it allowed her to feed her insatiable need, so her biographers report, for erotic attention, and to understand her way around desire, which is to say, around writing.

The Lover begins with that comment about her ravaged face and then corrects for the ravaging of age by presenting childhood, and experience, as ideals that continue to glow through the haze of history. *The Lover* is not an autobiography, but was received as disclosure. Duras became a huge star. Readers were eager to wade into a steamy vision of a colonial adolescence and to presume it was her life. As a novel it is no more conventional than her others, but its vivid compactness, the way it marbles and integrates the close and distant sensations and memories of a single consciousness, makes it a kind of artistic zenith.

The girl in the novel, never named, the "I" and the "she," is a little white "child prostitute," dressed in a man's fedora and gold lamé shoes, wearing a millionaire's diamond. The millionaire is a handsome Chinese landowner who takes her to a secret apartment in Cholon, the Chinese quarter of Saigon. Their liaison is forbidden, since he's not white, and all the better; a forbidden love is more urgent.

The first instance of a lover had appeared in the notebooks of *Wartime Writings*. He's called Léo, and he's not Chinese, but Vietnamese. He is ugly, scarred, and repulsive to her, but because of his wealth, and the pressure of her family, the young Duras pursues a relationship. She describes him as "truly pathetic" and "profoundly stupid" (which is how all suitors seem, whose affections are not requited). At one point Léo kisses her, and she's revolted. The scene is described almost like a rape.

In *The Lover*, the young girl has transformed into a pleasure doll. The lover bathes her, dries her, carries her to the bed. She's worshipped and adored and enjoys it, as power and as sensual rapture, and the reader feels the author's pleasure in this too. The child prostitute is gloriously self-possessed; her humiliations are society's hang-ups, not her own, and they only make her shine brighter, for the author and reader both, who collude in whoring her out. It's the "good" whoring, not the bad whoring—which may or may not have taken place but, either way, came first.

Later, Duras said the depiction in *The Lover* was her actual childhood, but those who knew her best suggest she had begun to confuse her fiction with reality. The affair in the novel is a "structure," as Lacan might say, a triangle of narrator, child, lover. Even Alain Vircondelet, the most credulous of her three biographers, calls the story a legend she invented, which, "having ripened during her whole life, finally became true." In *La Vie matérielle* she offers a corrective that seems only further embellishment: she says the lover didn't actually dry her after he bathed her with jars of water, but instead set her down on the bed *still wet.*

Rainwater. Bathwater. Rice paddies flooded by the Pacific: these are reflecting pools of an interior universe. Later, Duras poured the volume from *The Lover* into a new jar, *The North China Lover,* a new telling. But *The Lover,* a wisp of a book you can read in an afternoon, is the primal scene around which the other myths and reveries revolve.

Alcoholic, woman, writer—these identity-acts, the one who drinks, who lives as woman, who writes, seem to relate, all three, to a more fundamental, primordial action: the production of fiction, of experience woven into language. If we associate fiction with writing, what about with women? With drinkers?

The scene in *La Vie matérielle* when Duras encounters the "terrifying" man, who, she says, is living in her apartment and doesn't understand why she is afraid of him, was no mere daydream, but a full-blown hallucination brought on by delirium tremens from alcohol withdrawal. The man wears a black overcoat. She wonders if maybe he is there to remind her of "some immemorial connection" that has been cut but had been her "raison d'être" ever since she was born. She calls him a "master apparition." He's been in her house a fortnight, looking at her, unaware she can't understand him, and unwavering in his plea, whatever it is. This man presents to her a true nightmare, in which a lifetime of expression falls finally on deaf ears.

Eventually her hallucinations broke. When the man departed, Duras wept for a long time. Three years later, she found a way to speak of him, to Jérôme Beaujour.

Probably she even embellished the account a little, who knows, but in any case, how do you straighten the facts of a phantasm?

IS PRISON NECESSARY?

There's an anecdote that Ruth Wilson Gilmore likes to share about being at an environmental-justice conference in Fresno in 2003. People from all over California's Central Valley had gathered to talk about the serious environmental hazards their communities faced, mostly as a result of decades of industrial farming, conditions that still have not changed. (The air quality in the Central Valley is the worst in the nation, and one million of its residents drink tap water more poisoned than the water in Flint, Michigan.) There was a "youth track" at the conference, in which children were meant to talk about their worries and then decide as a group what was most important to be done in the name of environmental justice. Gilmore, a renowned geography professor (then at the University of California, Berkeley; now at the CUNY Graduate Center in Manhattan) and an influential figure in the prison-abolition movement, was a keynote speaker.

She was preparing her talk when someone told her that the kids wanted to speak with her. She went into the room where they were gathered. The children were primarily Latino, many of them the sons and daughters of farmworkers or other people in the agriculture industry. They ranged in age, but most were middle schoolers: old enough to have strong opinions and to distrust adults. They were frowning at her with their shoulders up and their arms crossed. She didn't know these kids, but she understood that they were against her.

"What's going on?" she asked.

"We hear you're a prison abolitionist," one said. "You want to *close* prisons?"

Gilmore said that was right; she did want to close prisons.

But why? they asked. And before she could answer, one said, "But what about the people who do something seriously wrong?" Others chimed in. "What about people who hurt other people?" "What about if someone kills someone?"

Whether from tiny farm towns or from public housing around Fresno and Bakersfield, these children, it was obvious to Gilmore, understood innately the harshness of the world and were not going to be easily persuaded.

"I get where you're coming from," she said. "But how about this: Instead of asking whether anyone should be locked up or go free, why don't we think about why we solve problems by repeating the kind of behavior that brought us the problem in the first place?" She was asking them to consider why, as a society, we would choose to model cruelty and vengeance.

As she spoke, she felt the kids icing her out, as if she were a new teacher who had come to proffer some bogus argument and tell them it was for their own good. But Gilmore pressed on, determined. She told them that in Spain, where it's really quite rare for one person to kill another, the average time you might serve for murdering someone is seven years.

"What? Seven years!" The kids were in such disbelief about a seven-year sentence for murder that they relaxed a little bit. They could be outraged about that, instead of about Gilmore's ideas.

Gilmore told them that in the unusual event that someone in Spain thinks he is going to solve a problem by killing another person, the response is that the person loses seven years of his life, to think about what he has done and to figure out how to live when released. "What this policy tells me," she said, "is that where life is precious, life *is* precious." Which is to say, she went on, in Spain people have decided that life has enough value that they are not going to behave in a punitive and violent and life-annihilating way toward people who hurt people. "And what this demonstrates is that for people trying to solve their everyday problems, behaving in a violent and life-annihilating way is not a solution."

The children showed Gilmore no emotion except guarded doubt, expressed in side-eye. She kept talking. She believed her own arguments and had given them many years of thought as an activist and a scholar, but the kids were a tough sell. They told Gilmore that they would think about what she said and dismissed her. As she left the room, she felt totally defeated.

At the end of the day, the kids made a presentation to the broader conference, announcing, to Gilmore's surprise, that in their workshop they had come to the conclusion that there were three environmental hazards that affected their lives most pressingly as children growing up in the Central Valley. Those hazards were pesticides, the police, and prisons.

"Sitting there listening to the kids stopped my heart," Gilmore told me. "Why? Abolition is deliberately everything-ist; it's about the entirety of human-environmental relations. So, when I gave the kids an example from a different place, I worried they might conclude that some people elsewhere were just better or kinder than people in the South San Joaquin Valley—in other words, they'd decide what happened elsewhere was irrelevant to their lives. But judging from their presentation, the kids lifted up the larger point of what I'd tried to share: where life is precious, life is precious.

They asked themselves, 'Why do we feel every day that life here is *not* precious?' In trying to answer, they identified what makes them vulnerable."

Prison abolition, as a movement, sounds provocative and absolute, but what it is as a practice requires subtler understanding. For Gilmore, who has been active in the movement for more than thirty years, it's both a long-term goal and a practical policy program, calling for government investment in jobs, education, housing, health care—all the elements that are required for a productive and violence-free life. Abolition means not just the closing of prisons but the presence, instead, of vital systems of support that many communities lack. Instead of asking how, in a future without prisons, we will deal with so-called violent people, abolitionists ask how we resolve inequalities and get people the resources they need long before the hypothetical moment when, as Gilmore puts it, they "mess up."

"Every age has had its hopes," William Morris wrote in 1885, "hopes that look to something beyond the life of the age itself, hopes that try to pierce into the future." Morris was a proto-abolitionist: in his utopian novel *News from Nowhere*, there are no prisons, and this is treated as an obvious, necessary condition for a happy society.

In Morris's era, the prison was relatively new as the most common form of punishment. In England, historically, people were incarcerated for only a short time, before being dragged out and whipped in the street. As Angela Davis narrates in her 2003 book, *Are Prisons Obsolete?*, while early English common law deemed the crime of petty treason punishable by being burned alive, by 1790 this punishment was reformed to death by hanging. In the wake of the Enlightenment,

European reformers gradually moved away from corporal punishment tout court; people would go to prison for a set period of time, rather than to prison as a place to wait for the physical punishment to come. The penitentiary movement in both England and the United States in the early nineteenth century was motivated in part by the demand for more humanitarian punishment. Prison *was* the reform.

If prison, in its philosophical origin, was meant as a humane alternative to beatings or torture or death, it has transformed into a fixed feature of modern life, one that is not known, even by its supporters and administrators, for its humanity. In the United States, we now have more than two million incarcerated people, a majority of them black or brown, virtually all of them from poor communities. Prisons not only have violated human rights and failed at rehabilitation; it's not even clear that prisons deter crime or increase public safety.

Following an incarceration boom that began all over the United States around 1980 and only recently started to level off, reform has become politically popular. But abolitionists argue that many reforms have done little more than reinforce the system. In every state where the death penalty has been abolished, for example, it has been replaced by the sentence of life without parole—to many people a death sentence by other, more protracted means. Another product of good intentions: campaigns to reform indeterminate sentencing, resulting in three-strike programs and mandatory-minimum sentencing, which traded one cruelty for another. Overall, reforms have not significantly reduced incarceration numbers, and no recent reform legislation has even aspired to do so.

For instance, the first federal prison reform in almost ten years, the bipartisan First Step Act, which President Trump signed into law late last year, will result in the release of only some seven thousand of the 2.3 million people currently locked up when it goes into effect. Federal legislation pertains only to federal prisons, which hold less than 10 percent of the nation's prison population, and of those, First Step applies to only a slim subset. As Gilmore said to me, noting an outsize public enthusiasm after the act passed the Senate, "There are people who behave as though the origin and cure are federal. So many are unaware of how the country is juridically organized, and that there are at least fifty-two criminal-legal jurisdictions in the US."

Which isn't to say that Gilmore and other abolitionists are opposed to all reforms. "It's obvious that the system won't disappear overnight," Gilmore told me. "No abolitionist thinks that will be the case." But she finds First Step, like many state reforms it mimics, not just minor but exclusionary, on account of wording in the bill that will make it even harder for some to get relief. (Those convicted of most higher-level offenses, for example, are ineligible for earned-time credits, a new category created under First Step.) "So many of these proposed remedies don't end up diminishing the system. They regard the system as something that can be fixed by removing and replacing a few elements." For Gilmore, debates over *which* individuals to let out of prison accept prison as a given. To her, this is not just a moral error but a practical one, if the goal is to actually end mass incarceration. Instead of trying to fix the carceral system, she is focused on policy work to reduce its scope and footprint by stopping new prison construction and closing prisons and jails one facility at a time, with painstaking grassroots organizing and demands that state funding benefit, rather than punish, vulnerable communities.

"What I love about abolition," the legal scholar and author James Forman Jr. told me, "and now use in my own thinking—and when I identify myself as an abolitionist, this is what I have in mind—is the idea that you imagine a world without prisons, and then you work to try to build that world." Forman came late, he said, to abolitionist thinking. He was on tour for his 2017 Pulitzer Prize–winning book, *Locking Up Our Own*, which documents the history of mass incarceration and the inadvertent roles that black political leaders played, when a woman asked him why he didn't use the word "abolition" in his arguments, which, to her, sounded so abolitionist. The question led Forman to engage seriously with the concept. "I feel like a movement to end mass incarceration and replace it with a system that actually restores and protects communities will never succeed without abolitionists. Because people will make compromises and sacrifices, and they'll lose the vision. They'll start to think things are huge victories, when they're tiny. And so, to me, abolition is essential."

The ACLU's Smart Justice campaign, the largest in the organization's history, has been started with a goal of reducing the prison population by 50 percent through local, state, and federal initiatives to reform bail, prosecution, sentencing, parole, and reentry. "Incarceration does not work," said the ACLU campaign director Udi Ofer. The ACLU, he told me, wants to "defund the prison system and reinvest in communities." In our conversation, I found myself wondering if Ofer, and the ACLU, had been influenced by abolitionist thinking and Gilmore. Ofer even seemed to quote Gilmore's mantra that "prisons are catchall solutions to social problems." When I asked him, he said, "There's no question. She's made tremendous contributions, even just in helping to bring about a conversation on what this work really is, and the constant struggle not to replace one oppressive system with another."

Of the ACLU's objectives, Gilmore is both hopeful and cautious. "I look forward to seeing how they revise their approach from the exclusionary First Step Act," she told me, "and to seeing how their ambitions, working in multiple jurisdictions, play out." In the last decade, prison populations nationally have shrunk by only 7 percent, and according to the Vera Institute of Justice, 40 percent of this reduction can be attributed to California, which in 2011 was mandated by the Supreme Court to solve overcrowding. Ofer conceded that the greatest challenge is to stop sorting who receives relief based on a divide between violent and nonviolent offenses. "To genuinely end mass incarceration in America, we have to transform how the justice system responds to *all* offenses," Ofer said. "Politically, this is a hard conversation. But morally, it's clear what the direction must be: dismantling the system."

Critics have been asking whether prisons themselves were the best solutions to social problems since the birth of the penitentiary system. In 1902, the famous trial lawyer Clarence Darrow told men held in Chicago's Cook County Jail: "There should be no jails. They do not accomplish what they pretend to accomplish." By the late 1960s and early 1970s, an abolition movement had gained traction among a diverse range of people, including scholars, policymakers (even centrist ones), legislators, and religious leaders in the United States. In Scandinavia, a prison-abolition movement led to, if not the eradication of prisons, a shift to "open prisons" that emphasize reintegrating people into society and have had very low recidivism rates. After the 1971 uprising at the Attica Correctional Facility outside Buffalo, New York, resulting in the deaths of forty-three people, there was growing sentiment in the United States that drastic changes were needed. In 1976, a Quaker prison minister named Fay Honey Knopp and a group of activists published the booklet *Instead of Prisons: A Handbook for Abolitionists*, which outlined three main goals: to establish a moratorium on all new prison building, to decarcerate those currently in prison, and to "excarcerate"—i.e., move away from criminalization and from the use of incarceration altogether. The path that abolition-ists called for to achieve these goals seemed strikingly similar to the original (if ultimately failed) goals of the Great Society and "war on crime" laid out by Lyndon B. Johnson in the mid- to late 1960s: to generate millions of new jobs, combat employment discrimination, desegregate schools, broaden the social safety net, and build new hous-ing. But the ravaging impact of deindustrialization on urban com-munities had already begun, and it was addressed not with vast social programs but with new and harsh forms of criminalization.

By the late 1990s, as prisons and prison populations expanded sig-nificantly, a new call emerged to try to stop states from building more prisons, centered in California and led by, among others, Gilmore and Angela Davis, with the formation of groups like the California Prison Moratorium Project, which Gilmore helped found. In 1998, Davis and Gilmore, along with a group of people in the Bay Area, founded Critical Resistance, a national anti-prison organization that made abolition its central tenet—a goal dismissed by many as uto-pian and naive. Five years later, Californians United for a Responsible Budget (CURB), of which Gilmore is a board member, was formed to fight jail and prison construction. CURB quickly rose to prom-inence for its successful campaigns, which, at last count, have pre-vented more than 140,000 new jail and prison beds (in a state where 200,000 are currently held in prisons and jails). CURB just recently succeeded in halting construction of a huge new women's jail in Los Angeles County, in coordination with several local groups.

Each of the many campaigns Gilmore worked on over the years was built from a different coalition of people who could be nega-tively affected by a new jail or prison. Her strategy was not to simply fight prisons directly and hope others joined in but rather to seek out groups that were already mobilized. Whether environmentalists who could be made to realize that a new prison would harm biodiversity, or local community members worried about a prison's impact on the water table or undeliverable promises of local employment, "whatever is already there, in terms of people who are organized, that is how to direct the work," Gilmore told me. "You have to talk to people and see what they want." In 2004, for example, there was a measure on the Los Angeles County ballot to hire five thousand new police officers and deputy sheriffs and to start expanding the city's jail. Gilmore helped organize a campaign in South Central and East Los Angeles, meeting and talking to people, getting them to ask questions and to express their needs. Did the needs of neighborhood residents coincide with the needs of the Los Angeles County Sheriff's and Police Departments? Did they want more police officers in their communities? The answer was no. The measure failed. "It was plodding work—organizing, and organizing, and organizing—but we won. We beat them back."

When the state wanted to build what it was calling new "gender responsive" prisons, abolitionists organized with people in California women's prisons. The organization Justice Now circulated a petition that 3,300 incarcerated people signed, to protest the new facilities intended to house them. A list of the incarcerated signatories—a twenty-five-foot scroll—was presented at the State Capitol, to audible gasps from the Senate budget subcommittee on prisons. The proposal by the state's Gender Responsive Strategies Commission was defeated. "It's not that everybody who was organized on these campaigns was themselves an abolitionist," Gilmore told me, "but instead that abolitionists engaged in a certain kind of organizing that made all different kinds of people, in all different kinds of situations, decide for themselves that it was not a good idea to have another prison."

*　　*　　*

By the time Gilmore began graduate studies at Rutgers University, in 1994 at the age of forty-three, she was a seasoned activist who had benefited from an extensive informal education with scholars like Cedric Robinson, Barbara Smith, and Mike Davis, the author of *City of Quartz*, who popularized the term "prison-industrial complex." Gilmore originally thought to pursue a PhD in planning at Rutgers, which seemed the closest to what she wanted to do: parse social problems in relation to the world we've built. Then she encountered the work of the influential Marxist geographer Neil Smith and quickly decided to mail her application to the geography department instead. Geography, she discovered, allowed her to examine urban-rural connections and to think broadly about how life is organized into competing and cooperating systems.

Gilmore received her PhD four years later and was hired the next year as an assistant professor at Berkeley. She wanted to call the first course she taught there Carceral Geography. The head of the department disapproved. "Can't you call it Race and Crime?" he asked. She replied that her course was not about race and crime. She got her way and has been developing the concept of carceral geography ever since, a category of scholarship she more or less single-handedly invented, which examines the complex interrelationships among landscape, natural resources, political economy, infrastructure, and the policing, jailing, caging, and controlling of populations. In the years since, Gilmore has shaped the thinking of many geographers, as well as generations of graduate students and activists.

I saw her ability to situate the problem of prison in a much larger political and economic landscape when Davis and Gilmore engaged in a conversation moderated by Beth Richie, a law and African American studies professor at the University of Illinois at Chicago, in a large church in the city, the three of them—black, radical, feminist intellectuals—seated in huge and ornate bishops' chairs. The event, organized by Critical Resistance, was crowded with South Side organizers, the youngest of whom were invited onstage to offer tributes to Davis, the most famous person in the room. It was all feel-good vibes, and then Davis turned to Gilmore and brought up the topic of private prisons. The tone in the room grew tense.

By now it has become almost conventional wisdom to think that private prisons are the "real" problem with mass incarceration. But anyone seriously engaged with the subject knows that this is not the case. Even a cursory glance at numbers proves it: 92 percent of people locked inside American prisons are held in publicly run, publicly funded facilities, and 99 percent of those in jail are in public jails. Every private prison could close tomorrow, and not a single person would go home. But the ideas that private prisons are the culprit, and that profit is the motive behind all prisons, have a firm grip on the popular imagination. (Incidentally, it isn't just liberals who focus their outrage on private prisons; as Gilmore points out, so do law-enforcement agencies and guards' unions, for whom private prisons draw off resources they want for themselves.)

Davis noted the "mistake," as she put it, in the film *13th*, by Ava DuVernay, in sending a message that the main struggle should be against private prisons. But, she said to Gilmore, she saw the popular emphasis on privatization as useful in demonstrating the ways in which prisons are part of the global capitalist system.

Gilmore replied to her longtime comrade that private prisons are not driving mass incarceration. "They are parasites on it. Which doesn't make them good. Which doesn't make them not culpable for the things of which they are culpable. They are parasites." And then she began a sermon on the difference between the profit motive for a company and how public institutions are funded and run. In her fluency on these subjects, a certain gulf opened between the two women. If Davis's charisma could be described as unflappable eloquence, Gilmore's derives from a fierce and precise analysis, an intolerance of vagaries, and it was Gilmore who commanded the room.

Government agencies don't make profits; instead, they need revenue. State agencies must compete for this revenue, Gilmore explained. Under austerity, the social-welfare function shrinks; the agencies that receive the money are the police, firefighters, and corrections. So other agencies start to copy what the police do: the education department, for instance, learns that it can receive money for metal detectors much more easily than it can for other kinds of facility upgrades. And prisons can access funds that traditionally went elsewhere—for example, money goes to county jails and state prisons for "mental health services" rather than into public health generally. "If you follow the money, you don't have to find the company that's profiting," Gilmore explained to me later. "You can find all the people who are dependent on wages paid out by the Department of Corrections. The most powerful lobby group in California are the guards. It's a single trade, with one employer, and it couldn't be easier for them to organize. They can elect everyone from DAs up to the governor. They gave Gray Davis a couple million dollars, and he gave them a prison."

The explicit function of prison is to separate people from society, and this *costs* money. Fifteen and a half billion dollars of the California state budget for 2019 went to corrections, and 40 percent of that goes to staff salaries alone, not including benefits and generous pensions. This is state-subsidized employment, not a profit venture.

Between 1982 and 2000, California built twenty-three new prisons and, Gilmore found, increased the state's prison population by 500 percent. If prison scholars tend to focus on one angle or another of incarceration trends, Gilmore provides the most structurally comprehensive explanations, using California as a case study. In her 2007 book, *Golden Gulag*, she draws upon her vast knowledge of political economy and geography to put together a portrait of significant historical change and the drive to embark on, as two California state analysts called it, "the largest prison building project in the history of the world." Were prisons a response to rising crime? As Gilmore writes, "Crime went up; crime went down; we cracked down." This sequence, and how crime rates are measured, have been heavily debated, but if this noncausal order is really the case, what was going on? Gilmore outlines four categories of "surplus" to explain the prison-building boom. There was "surplus land," because farmers didn't have enough water to irrigate crops, and economic stagnation meant the land was no longer as valuable. As the California government faced lean years, it was left with what she calls "surplus state capacity"—government agencies that had lost their political mandate to use funding and expertise for social-welfare benefits (like schools, housing, and hospitals). In the wake of this austerity, investors specializing in public finance found themselves with no market for projects like schools and housing and instead used this "surplus capital" to make a market in prison bonds. And finally, there was "surplus labor," resulting from a population of people who, whether from deindustrialized urban centers or languishing rural areas, had been excluded from the economy—in other words, the people from which prison populations nationwide are drawn.

Prisons are not a result of a desire by "bad" people, Gilmore says, to lock up poor people and people of color. "The state did not wake up one morning and say, 'Let's be mean to black people.' All these other things had to happen that made it turn out like this. It didn't have to turn out like this." Her narrative involves a broad array of players and facts, some direct, some indirect, some coordinated, many not: for instance, farmers who leased or sold land to the state for the building of prisons; the very powerful correctional officers' union, state policymakers, city governments, cycles of drought, economic crisis, and huge deindustrialized urban centers; and the lives and fates of the descendants of those who migrated to Southern California for factory work during World War II and after. Her fundamental point is that prison was not inevitable—not for individuals and not for California. But the more prisons the state built, the better the state became at filling them, even despite falling crime rates.

Golden Gulag has seminal status among Gilmore's academic peers and activist network, and also more widely—Jay-Z praised it in *Time* magazine—but certain sections of the book can be intimidatingly technical. Even Gilmore suspects that some who name-check it haven't actually sat down to read it. "The situation—causes, effects—are complicated," she told me, "and people want something that's easy." And yet when Gilmore interacts with people, whether one-on-one or with an audience, she is direct and accessible. She has a warm and effusive demeanor and is quick to laugh with people and bond with them. She speaks plainly and yet refuses to oversimplify. She gets people thinking about interconnections among larger structures that lead to the creation of prisons, and also interconnections among groups of people that might work together to resist the building of prisons—like environmental activists and teachers' unions.

It is in this manner that she organized in 1999 with both farmworkers and farmers ("in capitalist terms, natural antagonists," as she pointed out to me) to stop a proposed prison in Tulare County, and successfully persuaded the California State Employees Association (CSEA)—then a union of more than eighty thousand members—to support a campaign to oppose a new prison in Delano. "The guards could not believe that these public-service employees would go up against other public-service employees," she told me. "Even we were surprised." CSEA came to the understanding, as Gilmore recalls, that a guard is a state worker who has to have a prison to have a job, while state-employed locksmiths, secretaries, janitors, and so forth didn't *need* to work in prisons but might have to, if the guards' union got all the resources.

Despite a lawsuit initiated by a coalition of legal and human-rights groups, including Critical Resistance, and environmental concerns raised by a state senator, the prison in Delano did eventually open in 2005, but according to Gilmore it took many years longer than it would have without abolitionists' campaigning against it. "It got to the point where in Sacramento, they were saying, 'Just let us build this one, and we won't build any more.' That's how they talked to us, because they got so tired of us. 'Just let us do this, this will be our last one.' Before the ribbon cutting, the secretary of corrections said, 'This is probably the last prison we're going to open in this state.' He did not say 'because the abolitionists got in our way,' or 'the abolitionists organized all these people that got in our way,' but the implication was there."

"To understand Ruthie, you have to understand where she came from, what her family was like," Mike Davis told me. Gilmore was born in 1950 and grew up in New Haven, Connecticut, with three brothers in a household that she calls "decidedly Afro-Saxon," quoting the term that one of her mentors, the political theorist Cedric Robinson, used to describe the family of W. E. B. Du Bois. "Puritan determination was our thing," she told me. "I could not fail, because everything I did was for black people." Gilmore's family attended what was then Dix-well Avenue Congregational Church, which was heavily involved in the civil rights movement. "There was an ethos in my little church," she said. "Everyone needs to learn as much as they can." They had black-history lessons in Sunday school, where they were encouraged to wonder and ask questions. "If you made a claim, the rule was, you had to be able to tell someone *how* you knew it."

As a child, Gilmore secretly wanted to be a preacher. On Sundays, in the pew, she would imagine herself in the pulpit in preacher's robes. "Which is strange because I could barely open my mouth with strangers. So why I could imagine myself scolding and encouraging the masses, I don't know."

Gilmore's father, Courtland Seymour Wilson, a tool and die maker for the firearm manufacturer Winchester, played a central role in organizing Winchester's machinists. The only time in her childhood that white people came to the house was for labor meetings. She would sit on the stairs and listen to the men, who smoked and argued late into the night. As they left, she would peek through a window to watch them leave. "There was always a car outside that people had not gotten out of. It left when the others left." When she learned about Pinkertons, who spied on mine workers, Gilmore realized the men who parked outside her house were company spies, the equivalent of Pinkertons.

Gilmore's father had inherited a tradition of labor organizing from his own father, a janitor at Yale who helped to organize the first blue-collar workers' union at the university. Eventually Gilmore's father also ended up employed by Yale, where he worked to desegregate its medical school. "He was without question the leader of the civil rights struggle in New Haven," Mike Davis told me.

While Gilmore's father was not college educated, he was intellectually driven and encouraged Gilmore, a daddy's girl who showed much academic promise. In 1960, a local private school decided to desegregate before it was legally forced to, and sent letters to respected black churches asking about girls who might be "appropriate." Gilmore took the school's entrance exam, which was the same test it gave white girls, and passed. ("It was an easy exam. Like, for fuck's sake, what was all the fuss?") Gilmore was the school's first and, for much of her time there, only black student, and one of a small number of working-class students. She was miserable, but she learned a lot.

In 1968, she enrolled at Swarthmore College, where she got involved in campus politics. It was the year of occupations. She and a group of other black students, among them Angela Davis's younger sister, Fania, wanted to persuade the administration to enroll more black students, and Davis, on a visit to Swarthmore, gave the students advice. "She seemed so amazingly mature and knowledgeable to me," Gilmore said. "I was nineteen, and she was twenty-four. She had the Alabama style, talked slowly and deliberately, wore a miniskirt." Davis told them: "Figure out what you want, and stick with it. Make a demand."

In January, Gilmore, Fania, and a handful of other black students took over the admissions office. Gilmore invited her parents to come down from New Haven and offer political guidance. It was decided that Gilmore and her father, representing the group, would approach Swarthmore's president, Courtney Smith. When they found him, Gilmore, who was raised with formal manners, said, "President Smith, I'd like to introduce you to my father." Smith turned his back and walked away. Gilmore was outraged, but her father was casual. "He knew how to keep his eyes on the prize. What's it about? It's definitely not about *that*."

Gilmore's parents left, and the occupation continued. Eight days into it, Smith had a heart attack at fifty-two and died at his desk. White students alleged that Gilmore and her cohort were in the president's office yelling at him when he died (in reality, they were nowhere near his office), and there were rumors that these white students had threatened to get revenge.

At the time, Swarthmore, just like Yale, had a large number of black employees who performed the necessary if less visible jobs around campus, and these people, it turned out, had been observing events from a distance. "They decided to save us," Gilmore told me. "Cars pulled into the circular drive, and these black men got out and stood looking up at us, in the windows. We left with them. It all seemed magical to me. It was ontology put into action, that made it possible for folks to pull up in these cars and silently wait to rescue us, and we knew to be rescued."

The men drove them to a house where they bedded down for the night. The next morning, some people went out for supplies and returned with food and a copy of that morning's paper. In the paper was a picture of Gilmore's cousin John Huggins. He had served in Vietnam and been radicalized upon his return, becoming a founding member of the Southern California chapter of the Black Panthers. Now he and another Panther, Bunchy Carter, had been murdered on the UCLA campus by a rival political group.

Her cousin's murder was a personal devastation, if also a symptom of the politics of the time. (As later came to light, the FBI had infiltrated these organizations, in order to create the divisions that most likely contributed to this fatal encounter.) Gilmore left Swarthmore and moved home. Later that year, she enrolled at Yale and got deeply involved with her studies.

"Every year I had one teacher who was really good to me, interested in what I thought about and wrote," she said. One of them was George Steiner. Another was the film and drama critic Stanley Kauffmann. Gilmore graduated with a degree in drama before vagabonding across the country. She ended up in Southern California, where she met her husband, Craig Gilmore, and embarked on organizing work they've participated in together since 1976.

Gilmore has come to understand that there are certain narratives people cling to that not only are false but allow for policy positions aimed at minor or misdirected—rather than fundamental and meaningful—reforms. Gilmore takes apart these narratives: that a significant number of people are in prison for nonviolent drug convictions; that prison is a modified continuation of slavery, and, by extension, that most everyone in prison is black; and, as she explained in Chicago, that corporate profit motive is the primary engine of incarceration.

For Gilmore, and for a growing number of scholars and activists, the idea that prisons are filled with nonviolent offenders is particularly problematic. Less than one in five nationally are in prisons or jail for drug offenses, but this notion proliferated in the wake of the overwhelming popularity of Michelle Alexander's *The New Jim Crow*, which focuses on the devastating effects of the war on drugs, cases that are primarily handled by the (relatively small) federal prison system. It's easy to feel outrage about draconian laws that punish nonviolent drug offenders, and about racial bias, each of which Alexander catalogs in a riveting and persuasive manner. But a majority of people in state and federal prisons have been convicted of what are defined as violent offenses, which can include everything from possession of a gun to murder. This statistical reality can be uncomfortable for some people, but instead of grappling with it, many focus on the "relatively innocent," as Gilmore calls them, the addicts or the falsely accused—never mind that they can only ever represent a small percentage of those in prison. When I asked Michelle

Alexander about this, she responded: "I think the failure of some academics like myself to squarely respond to the question of violence in our work has created a situation in which it almost seems like we're approving of mass incarceration for violent people. Those of us who are committed to ending the system of mass criminalization have to begin talking more about violence. Not only the harm it causes, but the fact that building more cages will never solve it."

But in the United States, it's difficult for people to talk about prison without assuming there is a population that must stay there. "When people are looking for the relative innocence line," Gilmore told me, "in order to show how sad it is that the relatively innocent are being subjected to the forces of state-organized violence as though they were criminals, they are missing something that they *could* see. It isn't that hard. They could be asking whether people who have been criminalized should be subjected to the forces of organized violence. They could ask if we *need* organized violence."

Another widely held misconception Gilmore points to is that prison is majority black. Not only is it a false and harmful stereotype to overassociate black people with prison, she argues, but by not acknowledging racial demographics and how they shift from one state to another, and over time, the scope and crisis of mass incarceration can't be fully comprehended. In terms of racial demographics, black people are the population most affected by mass incarceration—roughly 33 percent of those in prison are black, while only 12 percent of the United States population is—but Latinos still make up 23 percent of the prison population and white people 30 percent, according to the Bureau of Justice Statistics. (Gilmore has heard people argue that drug laws will change because the opioid epidemic hurts rural whites, a myth that drives her crazy. "People say, 'God knows they're not going to lock up white people,'" she told me, "and it's like, Yes, they *do* lock up white people.") Once you believe prisons are predominately black, it's also easier to believe that prisons are a conspiracy to re-enslave black people—a narrative, Gilmore acknowledges, that offers two crucial truths: that the struggles and suffering of black people are central to the story of mass incarceration, and that prison, like slavery, is a human-rights catastrophe. But prison as a modern version of Jim Crow mostly serves to allow people to worry about a population they might otherwise ignore. "The guilty are worthy of being ignored, and yet mass incarceration is so phenomenal that people are trying to find a way to care about those who are guilty of crimes. So, in order to care about them, they have to have some category to which they become worthy of worry. And the category is slavery."

A person who eventually either steals something or assaults someone goes to prison, where he is offered no job training, no redress of his own traumas and issues, no rehabilitation. "The reality of prison, and of black suffering, is just as harrowing as the myth of slave labor," Gilmore says. "Why do we need that misconception to see the horror of it?" Slaves were compelled to work in order to make profits for plantation owners. The business of slavery was cotton, sugar, and rice. Prison, Gilmore notes, is a government institution. It is not a business and does not function on a profit motive. This may seem technical, but the technical distinction matters, because you can't resist prisons by arguing against slavery if prisons don't engage in slavery. The activist and researcher James Kilgore, himself formerly incarcerated, has said, "The overwhelming problem for people inside prison is not that their labor is super exploited; it's that they're being warehoused with very little to do and not being given any kind of programs or resources that enable them to succeed once they do get out of prison."

The National Employment Law Project estimates that about 70 million people, almost half the US labor force, have a record of arrest or conviction, which often makes employment difficult.

Many end up in the informal economy, which has been absorbing a huge share of labor over the last twenty years. "Gardener, home health care, sweatshops, you name it," Gilmore told me. "These people have a place in the economy, but they have no control over that place." She continued: "The key point here, about half of the workforce, is to think not only about the enormity of the problem, but the enormity of the possibilities! That so many people could benefit from being organized into solid formations, could make certain kinds of demands, on the people who pay their wages, on the communities where they live. On the schools their children go to. This is part of what abolitionist thinking should lead us to."

"Abolition," as a word, is an intentional echo of the movement to abolish slavery. "This work will take generations, and I'm not going to be alive to see the changes," the activist Mariame Kaba told me. "Similarly I know that our ancestors, who were slaves, could not have imagined my life." And as Kaba and Davis and Richie and Gilmore all told me, unsolicited and in almost identical phrasing, it is not serendipity that the movement of prison abolition is being led by black women. Davis and Richie each used the term "abolition feminism." "Historically, black feminists have had visions to change the structure of society in ways that would benefit not just black women but everyone," Davis said. She also talked about Du Bois and the lessons drawn from his conception of what was needed: not merely a lack of slavery but a new society, utterly transformed. "I think the fact that so many people now do call themselves prison abolitionists," Michelle Alexander told me, "is a testament to the fact that an enormous amount of work has been done, in academic circles and in grassroot circles. Still, if you just say 'prison abolition' on CNN, you're going to have a lot of people shaking their heads. But Ruthie has always been very clear that prison abolition is not just about closing prisons. It's a theory of change."

When Gilmore encounters an audience that is hostile to prison abolition, an audience that supposes she's naively suggesting that those in prison are there for smoking weed, and wants to tell her who's really locked up, what terrible things they've done, she tells them she's had a loved one murdered and isn't there to talk about people who smoke weed. But as she acknowledged to me, "Part of the whole story that can't be denied is that people are tired of harm, they are tired of grief, and they are tired of anxiety." She described to me conversations she'd had with people who are glad their abusive husband or father has been removed from their home and would not want it any other way. Of her own encounter with murder, she's more philosophical, even if the loss still seems raw.

"I had this heart-to-heart with my aunt, the mother of my murdered cousin, John. On the surface, we were talking about something else, but we were really talking about him. I said, 'Forgive and forget.' And she replied, 'Forgive, but *never* forget.' She was right: the conditions under which the atrocity occurred must change, so that they can't occur again."

For Gilmore, to "never forget" means you don't solve a problem with state violence or with personal violence. Instead, you change the conditions under which violence prevailed. Among liberals, a kind of quasi-Christian idea about empathy circulates, that we have to find a way to care about the people who've done bad. To Gilmore this is unconvincing. When she encountered the kids in Fresno who hassled her about prison abolition, she did not ask them to empathize with the people who might hurt them, or had. She instead asked them why, as individuals, and as a society, we believe that the way to solve a problem is by "killing it." She was asking if punishment is logical, and if it works. She let the kids find their own way to answer.

WOMAN IN REVOLT

"Hospitals, prisons, and barracks are like this. Once you're in, you're screwed. . . . You're sick because you don't understand their medicine," says Vincenzo Mazza as he encounters, and diagnoses with astonishing clarity, the repressive nature of life in Italy for a proletarian like himself in the year 1972. Vincenzo is a supporting real-life character in a film that primarily features a girl named Anna, whose last name no one seems to remember, or possibly they never knew it to begin with—never mind the fact that she is the point of absolute gravity and star of this nearly four-hour film, which bears her name and in which she, like Vincenzo, plays only herself.

In February 1972, Massimo Sarchielli, a professional actor living in Rome, had taken in Anna—sixteen years old, homeless, on drugs, and eight months pregnant—and let her stay at his apartment. He got the idea to make a film about her and called Alberto Grifi, by then an important figure in underground cinema. (His Bruce Conner–like *Verifica incerta*, made with Gianfranco Baruchello in 1964, was considered a groundbreaking experiment with found footage.) Grifi filmed reconstructions of Anna's past and of Sarchielli's initial encounters with her. "Where are you from?" Sarchielli asks her in one of these restagings, having approached an outdoor café table at which she's seated. "Cagliari," she says, which Sarchielli asks her to repeat, suggesting that impoverished Sardinia, of which Cagliari is the capital, is a bit off his radar.

These scenes take place where Anna had met Sarchielli, on the Piazza Navona—hangout spot for layabouts, loudmouths, *capelloni*, meaning longhairs, and all manner of the Roman lumpen that Pier Paolo Pasolini had once celebrated and fetishized, but by 1972 he had condemned them for not just their long hair but their *ugliness*. Anna, if the wrong gender for Pasolini's lost archetype, nevertheless refutes Pasolini's theory that the Italian underclass had experienced an "anthropological mutation," a physiognomic degeneration brought on by consumer habits. Anna possesses the beatitude of a Renaissance Madonna, as the camera acknowledges, gazing at her with a Warhol Screen Test persistence. With Anna, as with certain of Warhol's subjects we never heard from again, like Patrick Tilden-Close from Warhol's movie *Imitation of Christ*, the electrifying presence of filmed beauty and the obsessive gaze itself form a vivid and mysterious historical record, of "stars" who exist purely as stars, leaving no trace of lives continued off-screen, outside their moment of celluloid fame. These stars' only record is their record on film.

Almost unknown for the past four decades outside the country where it was made, *Anna* contains within it, as if under lock and key, seemingly every seed and secret component of that mythical and explosive era, the 1970s in Italy. After traveling the '70s festival circuit from Berlin to Venice to Cannes, *Anna* fell into obscurity for unclear reasons. (There is speculation that the film was taken out of circulation due to potential legal complications stemming from Anna's status as a minor.) Edited down from eleven hours of footage, *Anna* was the first film in Italy to be made on an open-reel video recorder (it was later transferred to 16 mm with the use of a machine, the *vidigrafo*, that Alberto Grifi invented). The format proved crucial to the movie's unfolding. As Grifi explains in an introductory sequence, video changed his relation to time. Time was no longer money, as with costly film, but something else: it was a matrix through which a filmmaker could at last move without restraint, capturing not just the quieter, seemingly insignificant *moments* of life but entire inconsequential stretches. In her relation to the filmmakers, Anna was afforded time and leisure, because she was no longer out on the street. And the camera had time and leisure to observe her, due to video's low cost. But as anthropologists understand, to observe is to contaminate. In this case, Grifi and Sarchielli were not merely observers. They presented themselves as Anna's saviors.

The plot—the "rescue" of Anna—was originally conceived by Grifi and Sarchielli in the spirit of direct cinema, along the lines of Jean Rouch's *Chronicle of a Summer* and Chris Marker's *Le Joli Mai*, and the neorealist concept of "tailing" as developed by screenwriter Cesare Zavattini, whom Grifi considered a spiritual mentor. But the directors of *Anna* quickly discarded their own script and let their interactions with Anna guide what the film would be—namely, a social experiment closer in a sense to Marker's 1968 *À bientôt, j'espère* (Be Seeing You), which documented the class consciousness of striking textile factory workers in Besançon, France. *Anna* chronicles its title character's circumstances as a homeless, emotionally troubled, pregnant teenager, and, reflexively, its own fraught production—and that is the sum total of the narrative, such as it is.

Much of the long run time is given over to interviews with various people on the Piazza Navona, each of whom weighs in with an opinion on Anna's situation. One young woman explains that the unions, like the Communist Party, won't help Anna because she isn't suitably proletarian—she's neither drug-free nor married nor employable. The young men say she's an untamable bitch. "She needs her head smashed in," says the one she identifies as her boyfriend. The only bourgeois person interviewed in the film, a lawyer, says with an amused air that it's against the law to take in a minor. She'd be better off in an institution (even as he says that he himself "prefers shotguns to institutions"). Or perhaps, he suggests, they can baptize the baby right there in the Bernini fountain on the Piazza Navona, and his companions all laugh.

Through these voices, Italy's ferment is heard. *Anna* was made on the heels of the Hot Autumn of 1969 and 1970, with its massive strikes at the big factories in the North and the deadly bombing by fascists of Piazza Fontana in Milan. This crime was wrongly blamed on an anarchist, Pietro Valpreda, whose imprisonment is discussed, in *Anna*, by the people who hang around in the Piazza Navona, almost all of whom have spent time in prison themselves, for charges they suggest are indirectly political (even the filmmaker, Grifi, had recently been in prison). The first warrants in connection with the leftist militant Red Brigades, an organization born at the Pirelli tire plants, had taken place a year earlier, in 1971. By 1972 the climate in Italy was repressive, and the people in the Piazza Navona joke that "out of every ten of us, there are eight policemen or spies."

All of them are from either Rome or Southern Italy and embody a culture that has no real historical relationship to industrial labor, to the North and its factories. They're an early iteration of the critical drift, in Italy, from factory-based struggles to a loose countercultural rejection not just of unions and traditional Left parties but of work. By 1977 this attitude would express itself as the impulse to *stare insieme*—to stay together and build a new life, operating against the reproduction of the class structure and pursuing the fulfillment of desires and needs that couldn't be met within the given state of affairs. ("The grass I want," as the slogan went, "doesn't grow in the king's garden.") The

denizens of the piazza declare flippantly that they're artists. "Make a painting, and Agnelli [the head of Fiat] will buy it for one million!" one young
woman jokes. These people on the Piazza Navona speak a confusing and
borderline-incoherent language, but one that is, within its specific and
dire context, logical: they talk about revolution, violence, and despair.

Unlike such ruffians, the Besançon workers in Chris Marker's *À bientôt,
j'espère* have properly proletarian desires: they want to go home on their
factory lunch break and eat with their wives. They want to have lives
outside the factory. Such workers had even taken control of the filmic
apparatus via the cinema collective SLON (Société pour le Lancement
des Oeuvres Nouvelles), cofounded by Marker in 1967, these workers
in effect transitioning from object to subject and ultimately sharing
producer credit with Marker. Anna, by contrast, isn't properly subjec-
tivizable. Not only is she subproletarian and Sardinian, she's a girl who
has trouble even wanting to live. She's not going to get involved in art
projects or protest movements. Instead, she's more like a weather vane:
a dark and anticipatory figure of the movement about to crest. She tells
everyone to fuck off. She tries to make phone calls with the receiver
upside down. She is sometimes catatonic. She isn't a participant when
the camera tracks the women's march in the Campo de' Fiori, where
Jane Fonda fleetingly crosses the frame (in the same year—surely not
by coincidence—that Fonda "crossed the frame" in the Dziga Vertov
Group's *Tout va bien* and *Letter to Jane*). In the Campo de' Fiori, the
women chant that the wife is "the proletarian of the family"—a priv-
ileged problem that has little to do with the concerns of someone like
Anna, who, to extrapolate from that formulation, would be something
like the lumpen of the orphanage.

And in fact she's just that. Orphanages were her early introduction to extrafamilial institutions, and institutions are what Anna, who bears on her wrists the marks of numerous suicide attempts, has recently escaped. She has spent her life in and out of them and knows intimately what the lawyer on the Piazza Navona, who said he "prefers shotguns to institutions," is pretending to call aid in suggesting she be returned to one. Nuns rubbed stinging mustard all over little Anna for wetting the bed when she was five, as she explains, and they whipped girls "of one or two years old." In *Anna*, institutions—mental hospital, delivery ward, jail—are totalizing. They are the horizons of her life.

The film, in its continuity with the world it depicts, renders itself similarly totalizing for both its subject and its makers, whose lives are embedded in it and not separate from the film's terrain. For Anna, the film is her only gig. She's lucky to be staying with co-director Massimo Sarchielli, a disheveled bachelor who looks after her, albeit with creepy solicitude, copping a feel on occasion and at one point delighting in the stream of milk she squeezes at him from her full breasts, which are readying to feed the child in her belly. Given that her only other option is the streets, she has little practical choice in whether to stay with Sarchielli and tolerate his groping, whether to tolerate the making of this film, which feeds off her vitality and her dissolution, in equal measure, as its mesmerizing agents. She's got nothing but this movie. And this movie's got nothing but her and her dire straits.

Grifi and Sarchielli weren't attempting to politicize Anna. They seem to hold out no hope of empowering her through the act of filming her. By the end of Marker's *À bientôt, j'espère*, a dialectical process of self-inscription has taken place that allows Marker, as filmmaker, to disappear. The Besançon workers form their own cinema collective, the Medvedkin Group, and by the time of the wildcat strikes of May 1968, they are behind the camera, filming. Anna, by contrast, is only a specimen, a "guinea pig," as Grifi referred to her twenty years later, in an interview in which he acknowledged the film's "poorly concealed sadism."

But in some ways Anna is less guinea pig than ghost, a symptom of the shift in the composition of the Italian Left, from the material conditions of the working class to a world of hippies, students, precarious workers, drug addicts, and other *emarginati* who would come to constitute the movement of 1977.

Anna's first act of revenge as guinea pig: she gives the entire crew lice. But this only brings on humiliation and paternalism, as Sarchielli forces her to strip naked and shower, berating her for having dirty feet. As she showers, the camera zeros in on her fingers absentmindedly playing with her own pubic hair, as if she were a gorilla at the zoo. While the crew deals with the lice problem, the film's electrician, Vincenzo Mazza, whose own views on institutions I quoted above, "leaves his post and enters the field," an intertitle announces. Vincenzo, a twenty-one-year-old former Pirelli tire factory worker who had participated in the famous strikes at Milano-Bicocca, steps in front of the camera to declare his love for Anna.

This moment, and the romantic relationship that ensued, Grifi later spoke of as an act of revolt on the part of both Anna and Vincenzo. Anna "wanted love," Grifi said, "not pity," although it isn't clear that pity was what the filmmakers were offering, unless it was a cruel, Nietzschean pity. Vincenzo, at the bottom of the cinematic hierarchy, was, according to Grifi, taking control of the apparatus by stepping in front of the camera, acting not out of the conditions of his role but from *desire*. Like the Autonomist movement that was about to unfold—joyous and incredible, but beset by the depredations of heroin and prison—Vincenzo's declaration is both moving and ominous. One senses it might end badly.

As if to confirm that the logic of the film is folded perfectly around the historical conditions of its subject, Anna has the baby on the day of a general strike in Italy. In what could be called her second act of revenge, she refuses the filmmakers access to the hospital. If up until this point the tireless video recorder has been an instrument of the directors' power, suddenly it, and they, are shut out. We never again see Anna on film.

"This girl's busted our asses," one of the intimate circle of regulars from the Piazza Navona says. Grifi observes: "It's clear that she screwed us over, from a film director's point of view." A discussion ensues about the exploitation of Anna. "You used her fully until the end," one woman says, "and now you're angry."

The filmmakers interview Vincenzo outside the hospital, in front of a wall of political slogans declaring the strike. He tells them, smiling, that the baby is a girl. "What are your plans?" Grifi asks. "I don't know," Vincenzo says dreamily. "It's spring, then summer will come."

The film cuts to Vincenzo again, hours later; the pediatrician has taken the baby because Anna is a minor and because she still has lice. With no guardian or husband, she cannot legally claim the child. Vincenzo, distraught, delivers a concise, poetic, and grim analysis of the situation, of a child born where "they only teach suffering . . . violence and all the rest," in a system of hospital bureaucrats who "end up not knowing themselves either, let alone others."

At the end of the film is another interview with Vincenzo, a year later. He is alone with the child, Anna having abandoned both of them. He says a woman chastised him for requesting help watching the baby while he worked. The woman told him children are a man's responsibility, and that Anna did the right thing by leaving.

While the women's movement was surely the most successful and lasting change wrought by Italy's convulsive '70s, the significance of Anna's refusal, her departure, baffles Vincenzo, even as he feels that the woman who yelled at him is right. Anna's "no," he says, *should* be a revolutionary "no." Instead, he says, her "no" is resignation and death, "a refusal of life and love."

Vincenzo has experienced firsthand an aspect of Anna's particular "emancipation"—she isn't mentally suited to be anyone's subordinate, much less wife—but he can't see that a life-affirming and revolutionary "no" makes as little sense for her as it would for her to march with Jane Fonda in the Campo de' Fiori. Anna is an avatar of a form of "no" that comes at the cost of everything, including her own child. He's despondent about everything, and it's tough to watch. But don't worry about poor, disillusioned Vincenzo Mazza and his plight of raising this child alone; he was murdered four years later on the Campo de' Fiori, I discovered by accident reading old copies of *Lotta Continua*, a widely circulating ultraleftist newspaper of the era. Vincenzo had intervened in a violent argument between a man and a woman and was stabbed. His killer, the brother of famous Spaghetti Western actor Gian Maria Volonté, subsequently hanged himself in the same Roman prison, Regina Coeli, where Alberto Grifi, the filmmaker of *Anna*, had done time.

And Anna? What became of her? The filmmakers, both no longer living, would never say. The last time they heard from her, Grifi later recounted, was while they were editing the film. She called, crying, from a mental hospital in Rome. She begged them to rescue her and also threatened to have them arrested for filming a minor. "All we knew to do," Grifi said, "was to record the phone call."

In the intervening years between making *Anna* and his death in 2007, Grifi was by turns reflective and defensive, blaming the 1975 audience at the Venice Film Festival for caring more about Anna on-screen than Anna in a mental hospital, and even declaring that this spectatorship itself turned the audience into the police—when it might be argued that the form of the film he and Sarchielli made, with its chorus of judging strangers, its strip-search shower scene, induced this effect. Sarchielli was more ambivalent about whether he and Grifi had exploited Anna, although the two apparently parted ways not over ethical disagreements but over the usual, banal problem: authorship (the Italian press treated the film as Grifi's alone).

If "Autonomia" referred initially to a withdrawal from all forms of organized left politics and, in particular, from the Communist Party, it would also come to connote an autonomous subject, one whose thought and actions transpire without the determinative influence of the state. Any movement or action called Autonomist is really an endlessly complex mesh and flux of various individuals coming together at various points for various reasons. To summarize Autonomia, then, is to banalize it. In this sense, testimonials by the individuals involved are crucial to analyzing and reconstructing this unique era of revolt, and *Anna* supplies a singular wealth of them, in all their coded and antecedent poignancy.

Even the film's own formal precepts—its dramatizations of real-life events, and the ghostly effect of its transfer from early video to 16 mm film, which communicates a once-removed quality—become unwitting aspects of *Anna*'s singularity, now, as a most curious time capsule, part graveyard, part glass menagerie. The film conforms to neither cinema verité's reflexive recognition of its own capturable moments nor direct cinema's claims to neutrality. The makers of *Anna* seem to think they are capturing the problem of Anna, not the seeds of revolt that are so palpable in the nihilism that lurks around the work's edges, in a vacillation between possibly productive anger and darker outcomes. Some of the people who appear in *Anna* would surely go on to become underground militants in Rome's Autonomia Operaia, while others would succumb to heroin addiction. One can assume that by the end of the '70s, most of the characters who ramble on camera wound up either fugitives, imprisoned, or dead—in any event, in places where no one would be filming them.

In the original credits provided for *Anna*'s screening in Venice, in 1975, every last character who walks through the frame—even celebrity cameos like Louis Waldon and Jane Fonda, who is seen for less than ten seconds—gets full credit. Even the lice get a movie credit. But Anna, on whom the camera focuses for most of the film's 225 minutes? She only gets a first name. Nothing else. If this omission reads as an index of her flight from institutions (or her attempts at such), it adds, considerably, to the mystery of her fate.

And if such a question, the fate of Anna, is a bit naive and crude, the film is nonetheless structured around it—as long as the question remains unanswerable. The film's object of fascination, what fades to merely a desperate voice on the phone, when she calls from a mental hospital, is its own sacrifice.

Then again, the unanswerable question, what happened to Anna, is Anna's third and final act of revenge, after giving them lice, and barring them from the delivery room: her fugitive retreat into invisibility and anonymity, a kind of renunciation that cannot be recuperated, pitied, objectified, stared at, or upheld as the altruistic (or at least formally innovative) work of other people. Anna's disappearance, a pure one—no one seems to know what happened to her, or to the child she had off camera—is her own.

LIPSTICK TRACES

Clarice Lispector had a diamond-hard intelligence, a visionary instinct, and a sense of humor that veered from naïf wonder to wicked comedy. She wrote novels that are fractured, cerebral, fundamentally nonnarrative (unless you count as plot a woman standing in her maid's room gazing at a closet for nearly two hundred pages). And yet she became quite famous, a national icon of Brazil whose face appeared on postage stamps.

Her first novel, *Near to the Wild Heart*, was published in 1943 and an immediate sensation, celebrated as the finest Portuguese-language examination of "the depths of the psychological complexity of the modern soul." She struggled to get her subsequent novel published, after marrying a diplomat and moving to Italy, then Switzerland, then Washington, DC.

Her return to Brazil in 1959, after divorcing in order to give herself over to her drive to write, commenced a decade when she was at the peak of Brazilian literary society, considered one of the nation's all-time-greatest novelists and contributing a weekly column (*crónica*) to Rio's leading newspaper. The Brazilian singer Cazuza read Lispector's novel *Água Viva* 111 times. Lispector was translated by the esteemed poets Giuseppe Ungaretti and Elizabeth Bishop, and in Rio she was a known and recognizable celebrity. A woman once knocked on her door in Copacabana and presented her with a fresh octopus, which she then proceeded to season and cook for Lispector in her own kitchen.

Lispector's philosophical fiction has inspired such dramatic devotion because people feel she is talking to *them*, about the most basic but complex human experience: consciousness, the alienating strangeness of what it is to be alive. She attempts to capture what it is to think our existence as we are in it—in the "marvelous scandal," as she puts it, of life. We are not a plain *is*, but an awareness of this is, which is to say totally cut off from the world by the human capacity to conceive our part in it.

Like Lacan, I blame language for this problem. Probably Lispector would too. But both of them, Lispector and Lacan, would agree it's our only recourse, and each called upon the capacities of language to an extreme degree, one building a set of psychoanalytic theories based on language, the other flexing language and punctuation in the interest of ephemeral and barely graspable truths, not because she was part of any experimental movement, she wasn't, but out of something more like solitary and desperate need. "This is not a message of ideas that I am transmitting to you," she declares in *Água Viva*, "but an instinctive ecstasy of whatever is hidden in nature and that I foretell." And elsewhere, "The next instant, do I make it? or does it make itself?"

An exhaustive biographical account of Lispector's mysterious existence, *Why This World*, by Benjamin Moser, was widely reviewed when it came out in 2009, and for a moment, many more people in the United States had read about Clarice Lispector than had actually read her work. Moser then oversaw new translations of five of Lispector's nine novels, *Near to the Wild Heart, The Passion According to G.H.* (1964), *Água Viva* (1973), *The Hour of the Star* (1977), and *A Breath of Life* (1978), which had never before appeared in English. The new editions are meant to be more faithful preservations of Lispector's intentional roughness and idiosyncrasies. She had a creative way with punctuation, and once wrote a novel that begins with a comma and ends with a colon. It's best to start with Lispector herself, but readers who encounter the novels will likely be driven to read Moser's biography as well, in order to know who is behind the curtain of that voice, which is so curiously personal and private, the inner voice of the quietest moment of rumination.

"Could it be that what I am writing to you is beyond thought?" she asks in *Água Viva*. "Reasoning is what it is not. Whoever can stop reasoning—which is terribly difficult—let them come along with me."

Moser speculates that her compulsion to write in the way she did relates to her origins in the miserable Ukrainian shtetl where she was born in 1920, her Jewish family's narrow escape from a wave of pogroms (they fled to Brazil when Lispector was an infant), and, when Lispector was nine years old, the death of her mother by syphilis, contracted when she'd been raped by a Russian soldier. Lispector had no memory of the Ukraine and rarely, if ever, spoke of that dire history. She was a native speaker of Portuguese and identified completely with Brazilian culture. One could argue that the omission of her origins in her work suggests that meaning lies there. But the compulsion to write, or really any compulsion, can never fully be accounted for in biographical details, whether by inheritance or life experience.

While a biographer's job is to construct theories of cause and effect, my concerns lie elsewhere, namely with those aspects of Lispector's personality and gifts that were possibly ex nihilo, or with those aspects that simply *were*. The most rudimentary questions of knowledge and being seemed to weigh on her in an unrelenting way. One has the sense that she really did get up in the morning and face the void. That this elegant and proper Rio lady wrestled with the question of how the hours pass, whether time is nature or human, and why we are so cut off from God, all while running her bath and making coffee in her percolator. She died early of cancer, at the age of fifty-six, in 1977, but left behind an astounding body of work that has no real corollary inside literature or outside it.

"I'm the vestal priestess of a secret I have forgotten," the narrator of *The Passion According to G.H.* says. "I know about lots of things I've never seen," Lispector writes in her own "dedication" for *The Hour of the Star*. In that same book, she writes that her task, in telling a story, is "to feel for the invisible in the mud itself." And, "You can't tell everything because the everything is a hollow nothing." The everything is the mud, the nothing that contains the something.

Lispector's subject, a grasping after the secret kept but forgotten, a kind of noumenal reality, "the invisible in the mud," is one that most writers don't even touch on. It's superspecialized work. She goes after essence, life stripped of what is the horizon and almost the whole of literature: the social sphere, family life, the contemporary scene, historical time, and, of course, romantic love. For Lispector, there is only the rubbed-down grain of existence underneath all that, even as her novels sometimes offer the tenuous webbing of narrative: a woman enters her maid's room and has an ecstatic breakdown/revelation (*The Passion According to G.H.*); a poor girl from northeastern Brazil comes to Rio and remains poor, dim-witted, and miserable, while the narrator, a writer, contemplates existence, misery, dim-wittedness (*The Hour of the Star*); a young woman with unusual gifts of perception contemplates life, her childhood, then marries, contemplates life, her childhood, and, vaguely, a love triangle (*Near to the Wild Heart*). But some of Lispector's work lacks even the pretense of a plot, like the great *Água Viva* and the even greater *A Breath of Life*. In both of those novels, Lispector dispenses with, or rather swerves around, narrative altogether, and gives her main subject—being—to us straight, in the form of aphorisms linked together. By some sleight of hand she manages to create a sense of forward motion without offering any kind of character development. She writes about thinking, what it's like to think, and this task is circular, because thought, while not language, is bounded by words, its only tools for expression. It could be said that this attempt to describe thought is the primary narrative propulsion in all of her novels, with the exception of *The Hour of the Star*, whose central character, Macabéa, is not introspective.

In all of her work, she seems to write in service to neither tradition nor vanguardism. Her prose reads like something closer to philosophy, but it's not philosophy. She isn't a scholar. She knows things from sun-bright intuition. What writer is her kindred? It's difficult to find a suitable example. Ingeborg Bachmann comes at the same problem of time, but from a different direction, when she writes in *Malina* that "today" is a word that "only suicides ought to be allowed to use," because it has no meaning for other people. Kafka is often mentioned, and Lispector appreciated his work, but their writing seems nothing alike. Kafka is a storyteller, no matter how unusual or abstracted the setting and events. Lispector is not. Kafka's characters are actors in life, who inhabit the world. Lispector's are not; they do not go here and there, encounter other people, have convincing spoken exchanges that result in effects on the main character and others.

The oft-mentioned Virginia Woolf is also a misleading comparison, given that Lispector's work is not stream of consciousness. "I want every sentence of this book to be a climax," she says in *A Breath of Life*, and even that self-reflexive admission is a kind of climax. In terms of mid-century currents and her own contemporaries, I don't believe Lispector was consciously experimental. There is no oedipal break being put into play, as with the New Novelists, no Oulipian limitation created in order to unlock something. If anything, there might be a link between her and the great Brazilian artists of her generation, geometric abstractionists Lygia Clark, Lygia Pape, and Hélio Oiticica. As Lispector says in *Água Viva*, "I want geometric streaks that cross in the air and form a disharmony that I understand. Pure *it*." When she was living in Chevy Chase, Maryland, in the 1950s, playing (or simply being) a housewife, Lispector's own contribution to the American Christmas tradition of holiday decorations was to cover a pine tree on her front lawn with dangling irregular forms in black, gray, and brown. "For me," she said, "that's what Christmas is."

It's important not to let cultishness stand in for the experience of her sentences directly, and yet the surreal mythologies of her life, like her wonderfully somber Christmas decorations, are a little too tempting to resist. Her dog smoked cigarettes and drank alcohol. She once held a dinner party and forgot to serve food. She said organ music was "demonic" but that she wanted her life to be accompanied by it. She wrote an advice column for a Rio paper with tips such as "Act as if your problems don't exist," and "No matter how French your perfume is, it's often the grilled meat that matters." Friends spoke of her "scandalous" cosmetics application, which grew more extreme after she fell asleep smoking and was badly burned. Her makeup evolved even further when, in the years directly before she died, she asked her makeup artist to apply "permanent cosmetics" monthly, while she slept.

*   *   *

The way she writes of vanity coheres with this odd detail of her permanent makeup. "What others get from me is then reflected back onto me, and forms the atmosphere called: 'I.'" Femininity, after all, is both utterly natural and completely fake. It's a mask. And it is the unifying impression a woman makes, the thing that keeps her gathered, recognizable to herself and others. "I wouldn't have been able to stand not finding myself in the phonebook," the elusive G.H. says. And so why not permanent makeup, for the woman who feels she is slipping, in more sense than one?

She was indeed beautiful for most of her life, with a face whose astral luminosity reminds me of topaz, her favorite stone. De Chirico painted her portrait, and there is the overhyped quote by Gregory Rabassa, translator of her novel *The Apple in the Dark*, which everyone repeated when Moser's biography came out, about her looking like Marlene Dietrich and writing like Virginia Woolf. No one would say that Albert Camus looked like Humphrey Bogart and wrote like André Gide. What Rabassa means is that she pulled off the unlikely feat, or so he seems to think, of being viable as both a woman and a writer. And yet I, too (wanting viability as both), have looked at her photos quite a bit. There is one in particular in which the inside of her arm looks so tender-soft that it produces a kind of confusion, a magnetic confusion that tells me I won't really understand much by looking at her photo, at flesh whose innocent appearance contradicts the mystical tone of even her earliest fiction (she had completed *Near to the Wild Heart* by the age of twenty-three). My favorite moment in all of her work is a childhood revelation of non-innocence in "Sunday, Before Falling Asleep," from her *crónicas*:

> This was when she discovered the Ovaltine they served
> in cafés. Never before had she experienced such luxury
> in a tall glass, made all the taller because of the froth
> on the top, the stool high and wobbly, as she sat *on top*

of the world. Everyone was waiting. The first few sips almost made her sick, but she forced herself to empty the glass. The disturbing responsibility of an unfortunate choice; forcing herself to enjoy what must be enjoyed. . . . There was also the startling suspicion that *Ovaltine* is good: it is I who am no good.

It is I who am no good. Hélène Cixous wrote famously of the Ovaltine moment, and it was through her writings that I originally found Clarice Lispector. Cixous wrote copiously on her work. She even took Lispector's reputation as "the sphinx" for a cosmetics tip, and made a habit of appearing publicly in full Egyptian eyeliner. Many of Cixous's writings on Lispector were pedagogical lectures given in the early 1980s at Paris VIII, whose effect in transcription is as magisterial as the eyeliner. I would have been better off reading Lispector directly, rather than in conjunction with the claims about her made by Cixous, whose own tone didn't wear off for me until I had occasion to pore over the new editions of Lispector's work.

"In truth she had always been two, the one that had a slight idea that she was and the one that actually was, profoundly," she wrote in *Near to the Wild Heart*, which seems to hold in it a code for the direction in which her work would eventually evolve. Its protagonist, Joana, apparently autobiographical, commits to married life just as she is overtaken by this second self, the one who "is, profoundly," who gives herself over to introspection.

Some people think *Hour of the Star* is Lispector's masterpiece. I am not one of them, but it is her funniest work. The protagonist, Macabéa, a wretched waif who comes to Rio from the slums of Recife, in northeastern Brazil (where Lispector spent her childhood), fails to find love or break free of ruinous poverty. A virgin who lives on hot dogs and Coca-Cola, she dreams of a house with a water well and wonders out loud, "Do you know if you can buy a hole?" She visits a doctor who recommends beer and spaghetti as a solution to her problems. She meets a whore turned madam and fortune-teller who "sentences her to life." Afterward, Maca is run over by a Mercedes. In this book of exceedingly spare prose, which was originally translated by Giovanni Pontiero, each word counts. This line, from Moser's new translation, "You do yourself in if you don't do yourself up," was translated by Pontiero as "Without a touch of glamour, you don't stand a chance." They mean the same thing but don't have the same aural effect (especially given that Lispector did not go for merely a "touch of glamour," but indeed did herself up).

If I cannot assess the translations themselves, since I don't read Portuguese, I know that the new rendition, by Idra Novey, of *The Passion According to G.H.* should be regarded as an event, based on the previous translator Ronald W. Sousa's admission in his own 1988 introduction that he didn't consider it a novel, and that his translation was "more expository in tone" than the original. Novey, by contrast, writes in her afterword about her own deep cathexis to the book. This new edition also includes an introduction by Caetano Veloso (probably the most famous person in all of Brazil, which perhaps gives him the leeway to make the absurd suggestion that Spinoza wrote the *Ethics* in Portuguese).

Lispector's most unrelenting and serious work, *The Passion* is a first-person account of a woman who passes into a state of intense exaltation—bathes in the Judeo-mystical *tzimtzum* of God's absence, but also partakes in the Catholic transubstantiation of God's presence, as if tasting the host—when she eats a cockroach. This is often described as "shocking," but it isn't, really. The severe philosophical austerity of her "passion" is offset by the bourgeois existence of G. H., who enters her maid's vacated room and begins this process of spiritual transformation when her eyes alight on the roach. There's a troubled racial overtone, a white woman and her absent black maid, a white room, a black cockroach, which she describes as looking like a "dying mulatto woman." Class is also significant: Lispector was obsessed with her maids and wrote about them in great detail in her newspaper columns. In picturing this haute-bourgeois character delivered into blessedness in a maid's room, I can't help but see an elegant woman with manicured nails biting into the creamy ooze of divine substance, the roach, as if into a bonbon. And yet there is nothing kitsch about this book. It is a precise portrait of an encounter with the secret to life: the nothing that subtends everything, the mud.

A Breath of Life, Lispector's very last book, edited posthumously by her loyal friend Olga Borelli, a former nun who was possibly in love with her, is the final installation, after *Água Viva* (which was also edited by Borelli from fragments and scraps), in a process that Lispector herself described as a "drying out." *A Breath of Life* is structured as a feverish dialogue between interlocutors who are really just vehicles for alternating epiphanies on life, and on the death that Lispector knew was imminent. These epiphanies are delivered one after the other in a book-length relay, a final and magnificent apotheosis of Lispectorisms.

> "One's incommunicability with oneself is the great vortex of the nothing."
> "When it's happening living escapes me. I am a memory of myself."
> "Life is very quick, when you see it, you've reached the end. And to top it off we're required to love God."
> "There must be a way not to die, it's just that I haven't discovered it."

"I can only accept that I got lost if I imagine that someone is holding my hand," Lispector writes in *The Passion*. And also in that book: "Holding someone's hand was always my idea of joy."

This kind of unabashed plea—to hold someone's hand—seems almost surprising amid all of the pondering on emptiness, which creates, in contrast, the impression of someone unreachable, imperious, and solitary, and she indeed had that reputation. But at the end of her life Lispector was not alone, and had a great friend in Olga Borelli, her most ardent admirer. Posthumously, Borelli put together *A Breath of Life* by sorting through Lispector's notes, which still smelled of the author's lipstick.

"It's a disgrace to be born in order to die without knowing when or where," she'd written in *Água Viva*. "I'm going to stay very happy, you hear?"

As if in answer to the simplest yearning in her fiction, as she was lost to the world—ours, and her own—she did not have to imagine someone was holding her hand. At the moment of Clarice Lispector's death, her hand was in Olga Borelli's.

BUNNY

met the painter Alex Brown when I moved to New York City from San Francisco, in 1996. We were set up on a kind of blind date by friends from his childhood in Des Moines, Iowa, whom I'd known in SF. Among his Iowa friends, Alex Brown had a certain legend attached to him. He'd moved to NYC, played guitar in various seminal hardcore bands (Gorilla Biscuits, Project X, Side by Side), produced a coveted zine called *Schism*, and almost immediately had an art career after graduating from Parsons.

"I'll be wearing a blue anorak," he said to me on the phone, so I could identify him when we met. We were more like immediate siblings than date possibilities for each other, and I repeated this line about a blue anorak to him for twenty years. He claims there was no blue anorak and what the fuck is an "anorak," anyhow? But that's what I remember. We went to see a Gerhard Richter show at Marian Goodman Gallery. I was aware that Alex's grandfather Alexander Lippisch was a famous Luftwaffe aeronautical engineer who was recruited to White Sands after the war. Looking at Richter paintings together, I immediately associated Richter's blend of formal precision and German trauma with Alex's.

From the gallery, we walked into Central Park. We sat on a rock and Alex told me that one day on a very similar rock he'd been on acid with a friend, the painter Alexander Ross. As they sat on this rock, tripping, they watched the artist Alex Katz approach a Sabrett cart and buy a hot dog. Three painters named Alex; two on acid, one eating a hot dog. They left and went to Alex Brown's place on Forsyth Street and, still tripping, walked into the scene of a dramatic drug bust.

Alex had moved home to Des Moines from New York just before I met him (he was back in town for a visit on our blind date). He'd been eaten up by the city for various reasons, including a telephone bill of something like thirty thousand dollars resulting from the fact that his neighbors were tapping into his phone line for their long-distance calls. He'd left in defeat but also a kind of triumph, because his art career was taking off, thanks to the passionate support of the storied and single-monikered gallerist Hudson, who ran Feature Inc.—then on Greene Street in SoHo, soon to move to Chelsea. Alex's paintings, meticulous renderings of pixelated or otherwise fragmented images, were each the result of hundreds or even thousands of hours of work, technically precise and meditatively, masochistically obsessive. His source material was imagery that had a "specific emptiness"—travel brochures, postcards, amateur pornography. "Turning [these images] into formal arrangements of color, pattern, and repeated form," he told Hudson in 1998, "becomes a sublimation, a ritual that allows me to enter their profound vapidity." The frame of mind needed to make this work seems to have required a big buffer of loneliness, which Alex successfully located in Des Moines. He could stay there and paint, and Hudson, whose gallery was entering its heyday, would be his lifeline. That was the arrangement.

Then again, maybe he moved back to Des Moines for the excellent programming at the adult movie theater on Fourteenth and Euclid, whose newspaper ads were regularly included with his letters to me, announcing either a live dancer named "ALEX," or one named

"RACHEL," and the one named Rachel had her name misspelled. He once sent me a drawing he found of a bunny rabbit in a waistcoat and monocle. He wrote, "This bunny has seen some serious shit." Something about the bunny's stoic face. We both knew exactly what Alex meant.

He regularly sent me mixtapes of rare recordings culled from his enormous vinyl collection and long letters that included his comedic gloss on the latest happenings in Des Moines—"there's a new titty bar in town in case you were wondering"—and summaries of the local courtroom drama over whether Amish buggies should have to sport traffic signals on their rear bumper. He sent me photocopies of the Art Bell newsletter, which he claimed was his primary news source, or pages from a David Shrigley notebook; a letter his mother wrote him at summer camp as a homesick child; collages he made me; missing children flyers that all seemed to resemble Alex, who himself had a preppy "lost child on the back of the milk carton" look despite his punk scene credentials; and Polaroids of whatever painting he was working on.

He was in New York a lot. He would tell me stories, like the one about the time he encountered a bunch of boxes on Fourteenth Street that contained *Screw* editor Al Goldstein's entire collection of memorabilia, which had just been put out on the street for some mysterious reason. We ran into people he knew everywhere we went, from legendary DJs on the Lower East Side to snobbish curators to guys from the hard-core scene, with tree-trunk necks and face tattoos. He knew a million different kinds of people who all put a claim on him of familiarity and friendship, and in every situation Alex was the same: with a slightly shell-shocked look, like that bunny in a waistcoat. Alex Brown might have been, in a curious way, the most popular person I ever knew, and he regarded his own popularity with hesitancy bordering on revulsion. He didn't quite know what to make of it. "It's so hard to go into the city," Chan Marshall sings in that one Cat Power song, "cause you want to say hello to everybody." I can't hear it and not think of Alex.

Alex introduced me to his gallerist Hudson, and Hudson and I became friends. Even though I lived in New York and Alex resided in the so-called Corn Belt (a teenage band of his was called Children of the Corn), he was the one exposing me to ideas and people, like fellow Feature artists Huma Bhabha and Jason Fox, who hosted parties where I met a lot of artists and listened to conversation that transitioned from Robert Ryman to Tom of Finland to Hans-Joachim Roedelius, and I didn't have much to contribute. Instead I took mental notes. Jason and Huma lived in Little Italy, and it seemed like the San Gennaro festival was in full flare every time I ended up at their house. When I think back on those years it's as if Alex and I are endlessly pushing our way in tandem under the colored lights, navigating past drunks and glass displays of fried shapes. Even if I was writing him a letter or updating him over the phone on some evolving situation, it's us moving in tandem under those lights. Like the year that Brigid Berlin called me regularly, at the offices of *Grand Street* magazine, where I was working, to tell me about her life as a daddy's girl and then a Warhol Factory girl, and I would summarize what she said and mail it to Alex in an envelope.

Meanwhile, Alex kept on painting. Started layering one fractured image over another, in the spirit of Picabia's "transparencies." Grew a mustache so that he could "get some respect," as he told me, while buying power tools at his local hardware store. Seemed to subsist on a diet of Sun Chips and Marlboro Reds. Every time he called me, he'd make up a story: "This is Larry Finstrom, Finstrom

Heating and Cooling: You guys are having a problem with your boiler?" "Is this dial-a-poem?" "Yeah, I need to rent a blow-up bouncy house?" Or he'd say his name was Bob and he'd met me at Jumbo's Clown Room and wanted to know if he could get a private table dance. Once we were on the phone when he got a call on the other line from Hudson, who was at a pay phone outside Alex's studio, in Des Moines. (I took this as a sign of Hudson's committed eccentricity, showing up, unannounced, in Des Moines, for an impromptu studio visit, but Hudson was apparently a follower of an ashram there.)

Feature quieted a bit after Hudson moved yet again, from Chelsea to the Lower East Side. Some artists lost confidence and left. Hudson asked his artists to have patience, stoicism, and a committed austerity on par with the anonymous tantra paintings he collected and showed. Alex devotedly complied. Luckily for him, he had a successful side gig touring with his old band Gorilla Biscuits, who sold out shows all over the world.

When Hudson suddenly died in 2014, Alex considered his lifeline cut. He was not going to do the social labor that many artists regard as part of the job, but he had a few solo exhibits in Paris and New York, including a mini-retrospective at Galerie Richard on Orchard Street. And he continued to make incredible work, work that really did require a kind of static life, or so he claimed. For years I had been collecting joke memoir titles that played on the ambivalence and solitude, but also the wry self-deprecation that I understood as his version of stability:

Table for Two for One: My Story, by Alex Brown
Duds and Suds: Clocking Time with Beer and Laundry, by
  Alex Brown (named after a Des Moines laundromat that
  sold draft beer, where he did his wash)

Friendly Fire: My Adventures, by Alex Brown

Hamburger in Paradise: One Man's Struggles, by Alex Brown

Can a Fella Get a Table Dance: The Diaries of Alex Brown

Married But Looking: A Life, by Alex Brown

And so forth. The list goes on, and appeared in my 2013 novel *The Flamethrowers*. Fiction is mysterious and can obscure its sources, even from its author, and I didn't realize until recently how many details, and how much of Alex, is in that book.

Over the years, Alex gave me two paintings. One is a pink and brown tree squeegeed in white and it's as good as any Gerhard Richter. The other is of the AT&T building on Church Street, a sublime and strange portrait of that concrete fortress that has in it a tinge of irony: it's the "communications" building, a structure that is windowless and blank. The painting is in my dining room. I stare into its vertical seams now, looking for cracks in its unyielding facade, and wonder, really for the first time: Where do people go when they vanish from the world? Until Alex Brown died suddenly of an aneurysm in January 2018, I had not felt the need to know.

THE HARD CROWD

"It's alright, Ma, I'm only bleeding."

You live your life alone but tethered to the deed of a mother. You live your life naked to the world and what it will pile upon you. And no, you will not avoid death. You won't survive it. And by you I mean not just Jesus, invoked in this Bob Dylan song whether intentionally or not, but you as in you, the person who is reading this. Someone loves you. That's not small. You suffer and she watches, living or dead. She can't protect you, but it's alright, Ma, I can make it.

In 1976, Jimmy Carter quoted a famous line from this same Dylan song: "He not busy being born is busy dying," except he stretched the line to make a point about patriotism: America was busy being born, Carter said, *not* busy dying. Italics mine. This was in his acceptance speech at the 1976 Democratic National Convention in Madison Square Garden. I watched it on television with my grandparents, in their bed, as the three of us ate bowls of "ice milk" from Carvel, whose packaging, like everything that year, was bicentennial themed in red, white, and blue. For Carter, a lifelong Christian, surely this idea of being born had an undertone of religious conversion, of being brought closer to

God, not just born but *reborn*: in a state of constant renewal, rejuvenation, renovation, change. I liked Jimmy Carter, a peanut farmer who wore denim separates on the campaign trail and was approved by my antiestablishment family. I was seven and could not have understood what Carter meant, what Dylan meant.

You are busy being born the whole first long ascent of life, and then, after some apex, you are busy dying: that's the logic of the line, its syntax, as I interpret. "Being born" here is an open and existential category: the gaining of experience, a living intensely in the present, after which comes the long period of life when a person is finished with the new. This "dying" doesn't have to be negative. It too is an open and existential category of being: the age when the bulk of your experience, the succession of days lived in the present, are mostly over. You turn reflective, interior, to examine and sort and tally. You reach a point where so much is behind you, but its scenes continue to exist *somewhere*, as memory and absence at once, as images you'll never see again.

None of it matters; it is gone. But it all matters; it lingers. The whole of youthful experience has slid away, the years and the people, the moments and feelings. In all that loss, a person continues to locate little tokes of joy from new and surprising places. Still learning, still becoming. Busy being born, *and* busy dying. You have a present, a now, even as you drag with you a snowballing bulk of what was. Sometimes you spike a new joy, you really do, and sometimes you hit an old one, and the more you've lived the more there are of the old ones.

I've been replaying film footage I found on YouTube that was shot in 1966 from a car slowly moving along Market Street, at night, in downtown San Francisco, the city where I grew up. The film begins at Ninth and Market and moves east through Civic Center, past multiple bright signs and theater marquees against the night sky, their neon, in pink, red, and warm white, bleeding into the fog. This 1966 view of Market is before my time and not quite the street I recall. It's fancier, with all this electric glitz. Neon is a "noble" gas. Whatever else that means it fits this eerie film.

Civic Center was where we kids went looking for trouble. In the daytime, cutting school to flip through racks of poster displays in head shops, and at night, going to the Strand, a theater where grown-ups would share their Ripple wine and their joints. This section of Market is on the southern edge of the Tenderloin, where the first among my friends, older than the rest of us, got a job, at age fifteen, working at KFC on Eddy Street. Her employment there seemed impossibly mature and with-it, even if Eddy Street, in the heart of the Tenderloin, scared me. She had money and the independence it buys. As soon as I turned fifteen, I copied her and got hired at Baskin-Robbins on Geary. Spent my after-school days huffing nitrous for kicks while earning $1.85 an hour.

At sixteen, I graduated to retail sales at American Rag, a large vintage clothing store on Bush Street that later, suspiciously, burned down. Business was slow. I straightened racks of dead men's gabardine, slacks and jackets that were shiny with wear, and joked around with my coworker Alvin Gibbs, a bass player from a semi-famous punk band, the UK Subs. On my shift break, I wandered Polk Street, past the rent boys who came and went from the infamous Leland Hotel. It, too, later burned.

The Tenderloin KFC is still there. It gets withering Yelp reviews, but what do people expect. The Baskin-Robbins where I worked is gone. You might think personal memories can't be stored in the generic features of a global franchise, and so what does it matter. I also figured as much, until my mother talked me into having breakfast at an IHOP where I'd been a waitress, for the purpose of a trip down memory lane. "Why bother," I'd said to her. "Every IHOP is identical." I was certain nothing of me could linger in a place of corporate sameness, but she insisted. We sat down in a booth for two, and I was plunged into sense memory. The syrup caddies on each table, which I'd had to refill and clean after each shift, the large iced tea canisters, sweet and unsweetened, the blue vinyl of the banquettes, the clatter from the kitchen with its rhythmic metal-on-metal scraping of grease from the fry surface, the murmur of the TV from the break room where girls watched their soaps. A residue was on everything, specific and personal. My mother sat across from me, watching me re-encounter myself.

This YouTube footage of Market Street in 1966 is professional-grade cinematography, perhaps shot for insert in a dramatic feature. I want to imagine it was an outtake from Steve McQueen's *Bullitt* but I have no evidence except it's around the right time. The camera, like the car we can presume it rides in, pauses at an intersection just beyond a glowing pink arrow pointing south. Above this bright arrow is "Greyhound" in the same bubblegum neon, and "BUS" in luminous white. This is how I know we are at the intersection of Seventh and Market.

The Greyhound station was still on Seventh, just south of Market, when I moved to San Francisco in 1979, at age ten. There were men sleeping on the sidewalk outside the station in the middle of the day. This is normal now, but in 1979, it was not. I don't remember this pink neon sign for Greyhound, but the station, now gone, remains vivid. It had an edge to it that was starkly different from the drab, sterile, and foggy Sunset District, where we lived. I remember a large poster just inside the station entrance that featured an illustration of a young person in bell-bottoms and a phone number: "Runaways, call for help." And I can still summon the rangy feel of the place, of people moving around who were not arriving or departing but lurking, native inhabitants of an underground world that flourished inside the bus station.

Next to Greyhound, up a steep stairwell, was Lyle Tuttle's tattoo parlor. Janis Joplin and the Allman Brothers had gotten tattoos there, likely while playing gigs around the corner at the Warfield, where I later tended bar. My oldest friend from San Francisco, Emily, a fellow Sunset girl, got her first tattoo at Lyle Tuttle's when we were sixteen. This was the 1980s and tattoos were not conventional and ubiquitous like now. There were people in the Sunset who had them, but outlaw people. Like the girl in a house on Noriega where we hung out when I was twelve or thirteen, whose tattoo, on the inside of her thigh, was a cherry on a stem and in script the words "Not no more." I remember walking up the steep steps to Lyle Tuttle's with Emily, entering a cramped room where a shirtless man was leaning on a counter as Lyle Tuttle worked on his back. "You guys are drunk," Tuttle said. "Come back in two hours." If anyone cared that my friend Emily was under eighteen, I have no memory of it and neither does she.

Later, I briefly shared a flat on Oak Street with a tattoo artist named Freddy Corbin, who was becoming a local celebrity. Freddy was charming and charismatic with glowing blue eyes. He and his tattoo-world friends lived like rock stars. They were paid in cash. I'd never seen money like that, casual piles of hundred-dollar bills lying around. Freddy drove a black '66 Malibu with a custom plate. He had diamonds in his teeth. Women fawned over him. Our shared answering machine was full of messages from girls hoping Freddy would return their calls, but he became mostly dedicated to dope, as did his younger brother, Larry, and Larry's girlfriend Noodles. Larry and Noodles lived upstairs and came down only once every few days, to answer the door, receive drugs, go back upstairs. Later I heard they both died. Freddy lived, got clean, is still famous.

The shadow over that house is only one part of why I never wanted a tattoo. I find extreme steps toward permanence frightening. I prefer memories that stay fragile, vulnerable to erasure, like the soft feel of the velvet couches in Freddy's living room facing Oak Street, where we all hung out. Plush, elegant furniture bought by someone living a perilous high life.

After the light changes on Seventh, the camera continues down Market, passing the Regal, a second-run movie house showing *The Bellboy* starring Jerry Lewis, according to its marquee. By the time I knew the Regal, it was a peep show; instead of Jerry Lewis, its marquee featured a revolving "Double in the Bubble," its daily show starring two girls.

The camera crosses the intersection and pans past the Warfield and, next to it, a theater called the Crest. When I was employed at the Warfield, the Crest had become the Crazy Horse, a strip joint where a high school friend, Jon Hirst, worked the door in between prison stints. The last time I ever saw Jon, we were drinking at the Charleston Club on Sixth Street, around the corner from the Warfield and the Crazy Horse. I was with a new boyfriend. Jon was prison-cut and looking handsome in white jeans and a black leather jacket. He was in a nostalgic mood about our shared youth in the avenues. He leaned toward me so my boyfriend could not hear, and said, "If anyone ever fucks with you, I mean *anyone*, I will hurt that person." I hadn't asked for this service. It was part of Jon's tragic chivalry, his reactive aggression. His prison life had begun after he'd stabbed someone outside the 500 Club on Seventeenth and Guerrero. Jon said the guy had insulted a woman he was talking to.

The camera moves on. It gets to the Woolworth's at Powell and Market, where we used to steal makeup. On the other side of the street, out of view, the camera has slipped past the enormous Emporium-Capwell, the emporium of our plunder, Guess and Calvin Klein, until, at least for me, I was caught, arrested, and booked, in the department store's subbasement, which featured, to my surprise, a police station and interrogation rooms where they handcuffed you to a metal pole in a locked cell, right there in the bowels of the store. I remember a lady officer with a Polaroid camera. I would be banned from the store for life, she said. This was the least of my worries, and I found it funny. She took a photo to put in my file. I smiled, big. I remember the moment, me chained to the bench and her standing over me. As she waved the photo dry, I caught a glimpse and vainly thought that for once, I looked pretty good. It's always like that. You get full access to the bad and embarrassing photos, while the flattering one is out of reach. Who knows what happened to the photo, and my whole "dossier." Banned for life. But the Emporium-Capwell is gone. I have outlived it!

The camera swings south as it travels closer to Montgomery, down Market. It passes Thom McAn, where we went to buy black suede boots with slouchy tops. Every Sunset girl had a pair, delicate boots that got wrecked at rainy keggers in the Grove, even despite the aerosol protectant we sprayed on them.

So many of my hours are spent like this, but with me as the camera, panning backward into scenes that are not retrievable. I am no longer busy being born. But it's alright; the catalog of a life's highs and lows regifts a person daily. Especially if she's figured out how to do a thing that takes all of her, for better or worse, into its accounting. That is what writing does. All the memories, the "material," it starts to answer questions. It gives testimony. It talks.

Years after passing the young hustlers in front of the Leland Hotel while on break from my job straightening dead men's suits, I became friends with one of those Polk Street boys. His name was Tommy. He was a regular to my shifts at the Blue Lamp, my first bartending gig, on Geary and Jones, at the top of the Tenderloin. This was the early nineties, and all the girls I knew were bartenders or waitresses or strippers and most of the boys were bike messengers at Western or Lightning Express, or they drove taxicabs for Luxor.

Tommy's face was classically beautiful. It could have sold products, maybe cereal, or vitamins for growing boys. And he was blank like an advertisement, but his blankness was not artifice. It was a kind of refusal. He was perversely and resolutely blank, like a character in a Bret Easton Ellis novel, except with no money or class status. He wore the iconic hustler uniform—tight jeans, white tennies, aviator glasses, Walkman. He would come in to the Blue Lamp and keep me company on slow afternoons. I found his blankness poignant; he was obviously so wounded that he had to void himself by any means he could. I knew him as Thomas or Tommy and only learned his full name—Thomas Wenger—when his face looked up at me one morning from a newspaper. Someone collecting bottles and cans had found Tommy's head in a dumpster three short blocks from the Blue Lamp. I don't know if the case was ever solved. It's been twenty-six years, but I can see Tommy now. He's wearing those aviator glasses and looking at me as I type these words, as if he and I are still in the old geometry, him seated at the bar, me behind it, the room afternoon-empty, the day sagging to its slowest hour.

There were times, working at the Blue Lamp, that I felt sure people who had committed grievous acts of violence had come and gone on my shifts. And in fact, I may have seen Tommy with the person who killed him, unless that's merely my active imagination, except I never would have imagined that someone I knew would be dismembered and have his head put in a dumpster. There are experiences that stay stubbornly resistant to knowledge or synthesis. I have never wanted to treat what happened to Tommy as material for fiction. It's not subtle. It resists, like he did, my comprehension. In any case, people would think I was making it up.

The owner of the Blue Lamp was named Bobby. I remember his golf cap and his white boat shoes and the broken purple capillaries on his face, the gallery of sad young women who tolerated him in exchange for money and a place to crash. Bobby's brother would drive his Harley right into the bar. Bobby lived out in the Excelsior, but the two brothers built an apartment upstairs from the Blue Lamp, for especially wild nights. I never once went up there. It wasn't a place I wanted to see. Sometimes the swamper, "Jer" we all called him, slept up there when he knew Bobby wasn't coming around, but mostly Jer slept in the bar's basement, on an old couch next to the syrup tanks. Jer's life philosophy was "will work for beer." He restocked the coolers, fetched buckets of ice, mopped up after hours. Drank forty bottles of Budweiser a day, and only resorted to harder stuff on his periodic Greyhound trips to Sparks, to play slots. (That Jer preferred Sparks to Reno was one of the only things about himself that he vocalized.) In addition to slots, Jer played video poker. We had a machine in the bar called Hot Point, which paid out to winners illegally in cash.

Whole parts of Jer, I suspected, were missing, in some kind of permanent dormancy. I wondered who he had been before he lived this repetitive existence of buckets of ice and Budweiser, day after day after day. He owned nothing. He slept in his clothes, slept even in his mesh baseball hat. I know. I saw. He lived at the bar and never went out of character. He was a drinker and a swamper. He said little, but it was him and me, day after day, night after night. A bartender and her bar-back are a kind of Platonic pair. And Jer had my back literally. After two a.m. closings, he would come outside and watch me start my motorcycle, an orange Moto Guzzi I parked on its center stand on the sidewalk. He insisted I call the bar when I got home. I always did.

These Tenderloin bars were human puzzles. There was one up the street that had a double bed in the back where a man lay all day like it was his hospice. You'd be playing pool and drinking with your friends and there was this man, in bed, behind a rubber curtain. Even the names of these establishments, all part of an invisible Tenderloin circuit, evoke for me this half-lit world: Cinnabar. The Driftwood. Jonell's. I remember a man, youngish and well dressed, who would come into the Blue Lamp and act crazy on my shifts. Once he came in threatening to kill himself. I said go ahead but not in here. Did I really say that? I doubt it. I can't remember what I said. A close childhood friend—whose name I just redacted and replaced with "Sandy"—came into the Blue Lamp asking me to hock her engagement ring for her. We had grown up together and she'd even lived with us for a while, with my parents attempting guardianship. They loved Sandy and love her still. Did their best. By the time she was looking to sell her ring, she had been living a hard life in the Tenderloin for a decade, working as a prostitute, and had become engaged to one of her johns. Who knows what happened to him. Maybe he bought a wife some-where else.

There was a girl who started cocktail waitressing at the Blue Lamp on busy nights when we had live bands. She told me her name was Johnny but also that it wasn't her real name. She was a recovered drug addict who missed heroin so much she started using it again over the months she worked at the Blue Lamp. She bought a rock off one of the

Sunday blues jammers and that is literally what he sold her. A pebble. He ripped her off, and why not. If Johnny is alive, which might not be the case, do I really want to know the long and typical story of her recovery and humility and day-to-day hopes, very small hopes that, for her, are everything? The glamour of death, or the banality of survival: Which is it going to be?

I didn't pawn Sandy's ring. I can't remember why. I did a lot of other things for Sandy. Tried to keep her safe. Brought her my down featherbed to her flophouse in Polk Gulch, the very blanket she'd slept under when she shared my room in junior high. Kept a box of baking soda in a kitchen cabinet of every house I lived in, so she could cook her drugs. She had a dealer who liked to eat cocaine instead of smoke it or shoot it. He would slice off pieces from a large rock and nibble on them like powdery peanut brittle. Sandy giggled about this idiosyncrasy as if it were cute. Anything she described became charming instead of horrible. That was her gift. She was blond-haired and blue-eyed and too pretty for makeup, beyond a little pot of opalescent gloss she kept in her jacket pocket, which gave her lips a fuchsia sheen. She'd say to my parents in her sweet singsong, "Hi, Peter! Hi, Pinky!" Even when my dad went to visit her in jail. Hi, Peter!

When I got my job at the Blue Lamp, I was living on the corner of Haight and Ashbury. Oliver Stone was making a dramatic feature about the Doors and attempting to reconstitute the Summer of Love for his film shoot. I disliked hippies and didn't even want to see fake ones, in costume. I can see now that this animosity may have been partly due to the outsize influence of my parents' beatnik culture and their investment in jazz, in blackness, in vernacular American forms as the true elevated art, even as my early childhood, in Eugene, Oregon, was loaded with hippies. By my twenties, they had begun to seem like an ahistorical performance: middle-class white kids who had stripped down to Jesus-like austerity, a penance I regarded as indulgent and lame.

Oliver Stone filmed on our corner, under our windows. Probably he made a deal with our landlord, paid him. We got nothing. So we entered and exited all day long. My look, then, was all black, with purple-dyed hair. My downstairs neighbor was in a band called Touch Me Hooker; their look was something like a glam-rock version of Motörhead. The film crew had to call "Cut!" every time someone from our building stepped out of the security gate. Our anachronistic barging interfered with their shoot. The next day the film crew was back. We put speakers in the windows and played the Dead Boys. I'm not sure why we were so hostile. There was one Doors song I always liked, called "Peace Frog."

In her eponymous *White Album* essay, Joan Didion insists that Jim Morrison's pants are "black vinyl," not black leather. Did you notice? She does this at least three times, refers to Jim Morrison's pants as vinyl.

Dear Joan:

Record albums are made out of vinyl. Jim Morrison's pants were leather, and even a Sacramento debutante, a Berkeley Tri-Delt, should know the difference.

Sincerely,
Rachel

As a sixteen-year-old freshman at Joan Didion's own alma mater, Berkeley, I was befriended by a Hare Krishna who sold vegetarian cookbooks on Sproul Plaza. He didn't seem like your typical Hare Krishna. He had a low and smoky voice with a downtown New York inflection and he was covered with tattoos—I could see them under his saffron robes. He had a grit, a gleam. A neck like a wrestler. He'd be out there selling his cookbooks and we'd talk. I wouldn't see him for a while. Then he'd be back. This went on for all four years of my college experience. Much later I figured out, through my friend Alex Brown, that this tough-guy Hare Krishna was likely Harley Flanagan, the singer of the Cro-Mags, a New York City hard-core band that toured with my friend Alex Brown's band Gorilla Biscuits. The Krishnas were Harley's vacation from his Lower East Side life, or the Cro-Mags were his vacation from his Krishna gig. Or there was no conflict and he simply did both.

There's a lot of the Haight-Ashbury in the recent four-hour Grateful Dead documentary. My favorite part is early in the band's history, when Jerry Garcia's old girlfriend says she dumped him when he got into bluegrass, back in his beatnik era. She found bluegrass music mechanical and uncreative. Jerry's studied fingerpicking on his banjo drove her nuts, so she ended the relationship. I watched the documentary on New Year's Eve 2018. At exactly midnight I got to the part where Jerry dies. Illegal fireworks terrorized my street in Echo Park as they announced Jerry's death on TV. The next week I told some people, "I watched that new Grateful Dead documentary on New Year's and Jerry died at exactly midnight." "Oh my God, he died at midnight?" is how most people reacted. They didn't get the joke. A Deadhead, my brother, for instance, would not find my joke funny, while a non-Deadhead doesn't even know that Jerry Garcia has been dead for twenty-five years!

Terence McKenna, the eating-magic-mushrooms-made-us-human guy, was way beyond the hippies. I once saw him give an eerily convincing lecture at the Palace of Fine Arts in San Francisco. He made a lot of prophecies with charts, but I forgot to check if any of them came true. Industrial noise musician Naut Humon was sitting in the row in front of me. He had dyed black hair, wore steel-toed boots and a "boiler suit" as it's called. Remember Naut Humon? I believe he had a compound at a former Green Tortoise bus yard down in Hunters Point. Only a human would come up with a name like that.

This was in the era of Operation Green Sweep. Bush—I mean H. W.—orchestrated DEA raids of marijuana growers north of the city, in Humboldt County. My friend Sandy, whom I mentioned earlier, got in on that. Profited. Sandy knew these guys who rented a helicopter and hired a pilot. They swooped low over growers and scared people into fleeing their own crops. They went in dressed like feds, fake feds, and bagged all the plants. Pot is now big business if you want to get rich the legal way. If I knew what was good for me I'd be day-trading marijuana stocks right now instead of writing this essay.

The Green Sweep debacle was after the paraquat debacle, a story first broken in *High Times* magazine. Carter's administration was giving paraquat to the Mexican government to spray on marijuana crops. Later, Reagan had paraquat sprayed from helicopters on marijuana farms all over the United States. Paraquat can be lethal. People who smoked pot that was laced with it might die.

I smoked laced pot a few times. Not from paraquat, but PCP. After sleeping outside the Oakland Coliseum to see the Who and the Clash, I was dosed. I was fourteen: in other words not a child. Luckily I'd been dosed before, so I knew what was happening even if I didn't like it. This was three years after all those people were stampeded to death at a Who concert in Cincinnati. When Roger Daltrey came onstage, the crowd mashed toward the front and I was lifted from my feet. There was a Mod behind me, very tall, in a fishtail military parka with a fur-lined hood. It was a hot day and I remember that he seemed like a robot, unbothered by the heat, and seemed not to notice me either. He shoved me forward. My feet weren't touching the ground and I could barely breathe. That's a strange feeling: like you're dying at a rock concert.

I always loved the Jim Carroll song "People Who Died." I get it. As a teenager I saw Jim Carroll and Ray Manzarek, the keyboardist from the Doors, do an awkward event together. Ray Manzarek played piano and Jim Carroll read poems about dharma and sepsis.

My first poetry reading had been Allen Ginsberg, at the Ear Inn in west SoHo. A free Saturday afternoon event I saw listed in the "Cheap Thrills" section of the *Village Voice*. I was fifteen or sixteen, staying with older cousins, and went alone. Drinking age in New York was eighteen and no one cared. I ordered a White Russian; it was a drink I'd heard of, and the idea it had milk in it appealed to me. I waited while Ginsberg came in with his retinue, or would it be cortège, a bunch of minders. They occupied a big table. Everyone waited while Ginsberg ate this huge omelet and a plate of fries. I think he also had soup. He started reading three hours after the appointed time. He read from a thick stack of pages. Read and read, as the discarded pages piled up with the dirty plates. I listened for at least an hour. Left, defeated, as Ginsberg kept reading. I walked out of the Ear Inn and into the rain, as taxicabs barreling toward the Holland Tunnel splashed me with greasy water. Poetry is for suckers, was something like my thought. Or, Ginsberg is for suckers.

You know who's a gifted poet? Raymond Pettibon. My favorite drawing of his is of a nude woman perched on a high exterior ledge of a building, about to jump. The caption reads: "I will my body to my father."

There was a punk singer in San Francisco who wore a nurse's uniform. She looked Hawaiian and her name was Pearl Harbor. Her band played with hard-core legends Agnostic Front at the Sixth Street Rendezvous one New Year's, but the show ended early because the singer of Agnostic Front got into a fistfight with a fan, right there in front of the stage. Pearl Harbor stayed pure of the whole affair, stood to one side in white stockings and a short white nurse's uniform, a starched white nurse's hat, as these brutes rolled around on the beer-covered floor.

This is from Charles Willeford's novel *Pick-Up*, which takes place in San Francisco: "Funny thing about these nurses. They all look good in clean white uniforms and nice white shoes, but they look like hell when they dress up to go out. I've never known one yet who knew how to wear clothes on a date. But when the clothes come off, they're women, and that's the main thing with me."

The narrator of *Pick-Up* finds work as a fry cook on Market Street in Civic Center. He doesn't specify the address but I see a slot where there used to be a narrow diner, just down from Fascination, a gambling parlor where my friend Sandy had a crush on the money changer the year we were in eighth grade. We wasted a lot of time at Fascination, watching gaming addicts throw these rubber balls up numbered wooden lanes, smoke curling from ashtrays next to each station. It was quiet in there like a church; just the sound of rolling rubber balls.

Those hours at Fascination, and many other corners of my history, made it into a novel of mine, *The Mars Room*, after I decided that the real-world places and the people I knew would never be in books unless I wrote the books. So I deputized myself world's leading expert on ten square blocks of the Sunset District, the west section of the Great Highway, a stretch of Market, a few blocks in the Tenderloin. My expertise is not just my knowledge but my permeability. The expert absorbs in excess to what is "useful" for a person to remember.

I never wrote about most of the people from the Blue Lamp. If I transformed them into fiction I might lose my grasp on the real place, the evidence of which has otherwise evaporated. The bar is gone. All those people have died. That might be why. Or perhaps a person can write about things only when she is no longer the person who experienced them, and that transition is not yet complete. The person who writes about her experience is not the same person who had the experience. The ability to write about it is proof of change, of great distance. Not everyone is willing to admit this, but it's true.

In this sense, a conversion narrative is built into every autobiography: the writer purports to be the one who remembers, who saw, who did, who felt, but the writer is no longer that person. In writing things down, she is reborn. And yet still defined by the actions she took, even if she now distances herself. In all a writer's supposed self-exposure, her claim to authentic experience, the thing the writer omits reporting on is her galling idea that her life might become a subject put to paper. Might fill the pages of a book.

I don't know where my friend Sandy is now. Under the radar. I've googled. It's all court records. Bench warrants, failures to appear. I wrote an ex-husband of hers on Facebook. He's raised her children by himself. No response. I don't blame him. Probably he just wants a normal life.

Wandering Haight Street with Sandy, as kids, the vibe was not good feelings and free love. It was sleazier, darker. We hung out at a head shop called the White Rabbit. People huffed ether in the back. I heard "White Room" by Cream there, a song that ripples like a stone thrown into cold, still water. "At the party she was kindness in the hard crowd." It's a good line. Or is it that she was *kindest* in the hard crowd? Like, that was when she was virtuous? Either way, the key is that hard crowd. The White Rabbit was the hard crowd. The kids who went there. The kids I knew. Was I hard? Not compared to the world around me. I tell myself it isn't a moral failing to be the soft one, but I'm actually not sure.

Later, skinheads ruined the Haight-Ashbury for me and a lot of other people. They crashed a party at my place. They fought someone at the party and threw him over the banister at the top of the stairs. He landed on his head two floors down. They had a Nazi march down Haight Street. The leader was someone I knew from Herbert Hoover Middle School, a kid who *had trouble fitting in*, as the platitudes tell us and the record confirms. He was a nerd, he was new wave, he tried to be a skater, a peace punk, a skinhead, and eventually he went on *Geraldo* in a suit, talking Aryan pride. Before all that, he was a kid who invited us to his apartment to drink his dad's liquor. People started vandalizing the place, for kicks. Someone lit the living room curtains on fire.

When I hear the sound of a Bic lighter's spark wheel, I think of something else: those red-cased Maybelline black eyeliner pencils we warmed over a flame for smoother application. Did you do that too? Warm the tip too much and it comes off in a blob on your eyelid.

Touch Me Hooker, the band my neighbor on Haight Street was in, included a guy I grew up with, Tony Guerrero. He and his brother Tommy lived around the corner from me in the Sunset, in the converted garage of their uncle's house. My brother skateboarded with them, was part of their crew until he broke his femur bombing the Ninth Avenue hill. Tony had an early skating career but gave it up. Tommy went pro. When we were kids Tommy and Tony started a punk band called Free Beer: add that to a gig flyer and you'll get a crowd. Free Beer. Free Beer played at the Mab—that's the Mabuhay Gardens, which had originally been a Filipino restaurant.

When I see people waxing romantic about the golden days of skateboarding, I am ambivalent. Caught up in the uglier parts. I think of former pro skater Neil Heddings and famed Dogtown original Jay Adams penpaling from state and federal penitentiaries, respectively. Or of a pro skater I won't name mistreating Sandy. An unmounted Santa Cruz deck of his design is still in my parents' garage, his name emblazoned on it in red. I think of people who were widely considered jackasses and died in stupid ways suddenly being declared "legends." I can't let go of the constant belittling, by skaters, of us girls as deserving of their slurs and disrespect, even though we were their friends and part of their circle. Guys outside the circle were "faggots" or "kooks." But look. Hey. I'm still friends with some of these people. And some of them contradict all of this. Tommy, for instance, for whom skateboarding was an outlet not for aggression, to destroy, but to be unstoppably creative.

As I said, I was the soft one. Maybe that's why I was so desperate to escape San Francisco, by which I mean desperate to leave a specific world inside that city, one I felt I was too good for and, at the same time, felt inferior to. I had models that many of my friends did not have: educated parents who made me aware of, hungry for, the bigger world. But another part of my parents' influence was this bohemian idea that real meaning lay with the most brightly alive people, those who were free to wreck themselves. I admired a lot of these people I'm describing to you. I put them above myself in a hierarchy that is reestablished in the fact that I am the one who lived to tell.

I was the weak link, the mind always at some remove: watching myself and other people, absorbing the events of their lives and mine. To be hard is to let things roll off you, to live in the present, to not dwell or worry. And even though I stayed out late, was committed to the end, some part of me had left early. To become a writer is to have left early no matter what time you got home. And then I left for good, left San Francisco. My friends all stayed. But the place still defined me as it has them.

Forty-three was our magic number. I see it and remember that I'm in a cult for life, as a girl from the Sunset. I scan Facebook for the Sunset Irish boys, known for violence or beauty or scandal. They are posed "peckerwood style" in Kangols and wifebeaters in front of Harleys and custom cars. Many have been forced out of the city. They live in Rohnert Park or Santa Rosa or Stockton. But they have SF tattoos. Niners tattoos. Sunset tattoos. An image of the Cliff House with the foaming waves below, rolling into Kelly's Cove.

Sometimes I am boggled by the gallery of souls I've known. By the lore. The wild history, unsung. People crowd in and talk to me in dreams. People who died or disappeared or whose connection to my own life makes no logical sense, but exists as strong as ever, in a past that seeps and stains instead of fades. The first time I took Ambien, that drug that makes some people sleep-fix sandwiches and sleepwalk on broken glass, I felt like everyone I'd ever known was crowding around, not unpleasantly. It was a party and had a warm reunion feel to it. We were all there.

But sometimes the million stories I've got and the million people I've known are pelting the roof of my internal world like a permanent hailstorm.

The Rendezvous, where Pearl Harbor performed in her white stockings and her starched nurse's hat, was down the street from the hotel where Robert Crumb's brother Max lived. We knew Max because he sat out on the sidewalk all day bumming change and performing his lost mind for sidewalk traffic. We didn't know he was R. Crumb's brother. We knew that only after the movie *Crumb* came out. I'm not sure if I'll ever watch that movie again. Too sad.

Harley from the Cro-Mags is a fixed memory from Berkeley, but whatever he wanted never registered. Maybe he just wanted to sell me vegetarian cookbooks. This was a few years after he almost held up the artist Richard Prince, who lived in Harley's East Village building. Richard said, "Hey, pal, I'm your neighbor. Go rob someone else." (Harley denies that this happened.)

Richard Prince got his start at the same gallery where Alex Brown showed his work, Feature. There was another artist at Feature who had supposedly painted on sleeping bags once upon a time. I actually never saw the Sleeping Bag Paintings. I heard about them and that was enough. There'd be a moment in a late-night conversation when someone would inevitably mention them. We'd all nod. "Yeah, the Sleeping Bag Paintings." Robert Rauschenberg made a painting on a quilted blanket; that's pretty close and way earlier: 1955. The blanket belonged to Dorothea Rockburne. I guess he borrowed it. A quilt is more traditional and American, while sleeping bags are for hippies, for transients with no respect.

I thought, as I wrote the previous paragraph, that I could be making this stuff up, that no one had painted on sleeping bags, a too-slippery fabric. But last night I ran into the guy who made them. I hadn't seen him in twenty years. He confirmed. Not just the paintings but himself and also me. We exist.

The things I've seen and the people I've known: maybe it just can't matter to you. That's what Jimmy Stewart says to Kim Novak in *Vertigo*. He wants Novak's character Judy to wear her hair like the unreachable Madeleine did. He wants Judy to be a Pacific Heights class act and not a downtown department store tramp.

"Judy, please, it can't matter to *you*."

Outrageous. He's talking about a woman's own hair. Of course it matters to her.

I'm talking about my own life. Which not only can't matter to you, it might bore you.

So: Get your own gig. Make your litany, as I have just made mine. Keep your tally. Mind your dead, and your living, and you can bore me.

ACKNOWLEDGMENTS

This book was Jason Smith's idea. I owe much gratitude also to my agent, Susan Golomb, and my editor, Nan Graham; to Claire Gutierrez at the *New York Times Magazine*, whose feedback I'd like to think has made me a better writer, and the same goes for the editorial guidance of *Artforum*'s Elizabeth Schambelan. I thank David Velasco, Michael Miller, Hedi El Kholti, Nicole Rudick, Scott Rothkopf, Eric Banks, and all the editors I worked with on these essays; and Katie Monaghan, Roz Lippel, Tamar McCollum, Sabrina Pyun, Katie Rizzo, and everyone at Scribner. James Lickwar vetted and confirmed details about the Cabo 1000 and the year we rode in it. Emily Goldman did the same for the title essay, pertaining to our SF. Benjamin Weissman brought me to Los Angeles to read "Girl on a Motorcycle" when I was unpublished, unproven, unknown. Ayelet Waldman, Michael Chabon, and Moriel Rothman-Zecher brought me to Palestine. Thomas Demand and Alexander Kluge brought me to Venice. Armand Powell Croft III brought me to Oktoberfest, and it wasn't fun at all but I thank him for a lifetime of friendship and for helping me buy my first motorcycle. Gale Harold and Chris Beach confirmed details of our time working for Bill Graham Presents. Anna Moï unknotted debates of place name and family name that are misunderstood even by the French. Daniele Balicco and Maria Teresa Carbone, Jasper Bernes and Joshua Clover, gave me occasions for eulogizing Nanni Balestrini. I thank Alex Brown's family, his friends, and his band Gorilla Biscuits for keeping his memory alive, and Alexander Ross for verifying details. I thank Hiba Nababta and the late Baha Nababta for their hospitality and kindness, and Craig and Ruthie Gilmore for theirs. "The Hard Crowd" was originally the title of an essay I wrote for Richard Prince; it has transformed into a different thing, but in spirit Richard is still there. Lastly, I thank Cynthia Mitchell for verifying everything including the noumenon, and Remy Kushner for his wisdom and good humor.

A version of "Girl on a Motorcycle" appeared in *She's a Bad Motorcycle: Writers on Riding* (Da Capo, 2001).

"We Are Orphans Here" appeared in the *New York Times Magazine*, December 1, 2016; *Kingdom of Olives and Ash* (HarperCollins, 2017), edited by Michael Chabon and Ayelet Waldman; and Leslie Jamison, ed., *The Best American Essays 2017* (Houghton Mifflin Harcourt, 2017).

"Earth Angel: Denis Johnson's Final Book of Fiction," *Bookforum* (February/March 2018).

"In the Company of Truckers," *New York Times Magazine*, February 19, 2014.

"Bad Captains," *London Review of Books*, no. 22 (January 2015).

"Happy Hour," *Jeff Koons: A Retrospective*, Whitney Museum of American Art, 2014.

"Tramping in the Byways" appeared as the afterword to *How I Became One of the Invisible*, by David Rattray (Semiotext(e), 2019).

"Flying Cars," from *Matthew Porter: The Heights* (Aperture Books, 2019).

"Picture-Book Horses" appeared as the introduction to *The Border Trilogy* by Cormac McCarthy (Picador UK, 2018).

"Not with the Band": a much shorter, altered version originally appeared in *Vogue*, May 2018.

A version of "Made to Burn" originally appeared in the *Paris Review*, issue 203 (Winter 2012).

"Popular Mechanics" is developed and lengthened from a preface to *We Want Everything* by Nanni Balestrini (Verso, 2016) and "Nanni Balestrini, 1935–2019," *Commune Magazine*, fall 2019.

"The Sinking of the HMS Bounty" is a revised and extended version of an essay from a catalog for an exhibition by Thomas Demand, Alexander Kluge, and Anna Viebrock, *The Boat Is Leaking. The Captain Lied.*, Fondazione Prada, 2017.

"Duras with an *S*" is developed and lengthened from a foreword to *The Lover, Wartime Notebooks, Practicalities* by Marguerite Duras, Everyman's Library edition (Alfred A. Knopf, 2018); it also appeared as "A Man and a Woman, Say What You Like, They're Different," *New Yorker* pageturner, November 10, 2017.

"Is Prison Necessary?," *New York Times Magazine*, April 17, 2019.

"Woman in Revolt," *Artforum* 51, no. 3 (November 2012).

"Lipstick Traces," *Bookforum* (December/January 2013).

"Bunny" is developed and lengthened from "Passages: Alex Brown," *Artforum* 57, no. 8 (April 2019).

IMAGE CREDITS

Detail from the cover of *I Volsci* (March 1980), issue 10, courtesy of London School of Economics Red Notes Archive.

Tano D'Amico, *At the Gates of the University*, 1977, © Yale University's Beinecke Rare Book & Manuscript Library.

Cover of *Mara e le altre*, courtesy of Evan Calder Williams.

Portfolio design by Charlotte Strick for the *Paris Review*, 2012.

ABOUT THE AUTHOR

Rachel Kushner is the author of the internationally acclaimed novels *The Mars Room*, *The Flamethrowers*, and *Telex from Cuba*, as well as a book of short stories, *The Strange Case of Rachel K*. She has won the Prix Médicis and been a finalist for the Booker Prize, the National Book Critics Circle Award, and was twice a finalist for the National Book Award in Fiction. She is a Guggenheim Foundation Fellow and the recipient of the Harold D. Vursell Memorial Award from the American Academy of Arts and Letters. Her books have been translated into twenty-six languages.